SMOKING MEAT

Will Fleischman

CONTENTS

COOKING LOW AND SLOW

The artistry and technique of smoking meats takes a delicate blend of patience and skill. Low temperatures and long cooking times test our ability to control fire, while we have to be willing to overcome our need to "see things happening" and just have confidence in the process. Successfully cooking low and slow barbecue demands learning what's necessary for a good (and safe) smoke, as well as understanding the meats you're smoking and how they'll behave in the smoker.

COOKING with SMOKE

Learning how the process of smoking works is the first step in discovering how to smoke foods in the right way. A little know-how will help you to maximize your chance of success, as well as to trouble-shoot and solve many common problems that can happen as you cook using this ancient technique.

SMOKING VS. GRILLING

What's the difference?

While both smoking and grilling over a barbecue use fire and can impart a smoky flavour to meats, they differ greatly when it comes to cooking time and the manner in which meats cook. A grill sears and caramelizes proteins using high, direct heat, whereas smoking uses indirect heat and lower temperatures to caramelize but not sear the meat. Over a grill, the cooking is done in mere minutes; on a smoker, you rarely spend less than an hour cooking meats. Ultimately, cooking with smoke requires patience and practice.

WHAT ARE THE BENEFITS OF THE SMOKE?

While grilling over a barbecue may impart some flavours to meat, smoking gives much deeper, more intensive flavours that can only be attained over a long, slow cook. Additionally, the compounds in wood smoke – specifically, the phenols and phenolic compounds – act as antimicrobials that slow bacterial growth and prevent meat from turning rancid. Wood smoke also contains antioxidants that help to preserve meat.

Smoking gives meats such as these jerk-rubbed chicken wings a deeper, more complex flavour than they would get over a grill.

THE SCIENCE OF SMOKING

How smoking actually cooks

Smoking cooks cuts of meat by exposing them to low-temperature heat (93–150°C / 200–300°F). The smoke coming from smouldering wood over a fire lends flavours to the meat. While a fire isn't needed to smoulder wood – even an electric heat source can effectively produce smoke from a small amount of water-soaked wood chips – most professionals agree that a fire is needed to create the bold tastes you want from smoked foods.

Cold smoking vs. hot smoking

There are two types of smoking: *cold smoking* and *hot smoking.* Cold smoking is the process of flavouring foods at temperatures less than 49°C (120°F). Typically, items for cold smoking have already been cured, such as bacon or salmon. However, cold smoking isn't limited to traditional foods. These days, barley and hops are smoked for beers to give them a subtle smoke flavour, and you can even smoke filtered water to make smoky ice cubes for cocktails.

Hot smoking, on the other hand, is a process that simultaneously cooks and flavours foods and is performed at higher temperatures (93–150°C / 200–300°F). Hot smoking is typically reserved for foods that have not been previously cured, such as fresh cuts of beef, pork, or poultry, that require a full cooking time.

Air flow and temperature

Because hot air rises quickly, capturing the movement of hot air from the firebox is necessary for even cooking. A properly designed smoker allows air to enter the firebox and moves it to the cooking chamber, where it fuels the fire and helps burn the wood. This then creates the smoke and heat that cooks and flavours the food. Because of this, consistent air flow is essential to smoking success. The internal temperature of meat is slowly raised by the circulating warm air. While the outside parts heat up quickly, the core temperature of the thickest parts – especially in larger cuts – takes much longer to rise.

The low temperatures used in smoking mean it takes longer for the internal temperature of meat to rise, for the connective tissue and fats to break down, and for the meat to become tender. Because of this, maintaining proper air flow will help keep the fire burning and the smoke flowing, as well as keep the temperature at a consistent level.

> **Controlling temperature and air flow during the smoking process is important. If you're not careful, exposing less fatty or delicate meats to low-temperature heat can lead to it drying out.**

Cabinet smokers have easy-access fireboxes that allow you to add more wood and thus to keep the temperature stable.

CORE PRINCIPLES

Before you start down the path to smoking, there are some basic principles you need to learn. Setting yourself up with the right equipment, as well as mastering some essential techniques, will increase your chances of success and get you to a point where you're getting the results you want on a consistent basis.

1. START WITH A GOOD PIT

One of the early mistakes I made when first learning to smoke meats was purchasing a cheap, poorly insulated smoker that had no insulation around the cooking chamber and a very small pan to hold coals and additional wood. It wasn't sealed, and it allowed even the slightest breeze to move the temperature up by as much as 10°C (20°F). Unsurprisingly, with this leaky smoker I fought a constant battle to try to increase or reduce the temperature, resulting in poor meals.

Every firepit has its own unique personality. But the better the quality of the pit, the less you'll have to worry about outside factors affecting your smoked meats. When you buy a pit, consider how much space you have to store the smoker, also how much food you'll be smoking at any given time, and what kind of food you'll typically be smoking. Buy the best smoker you can afford, and avoid cheaply built models that will only give you disappointing food.

An offset smoker has a very simple design, making it ideal for enthusiasts and anyone new to smoking. Just be sure to invest in a high-quality model, as cheaper offset smokers will heat your meats inefficiently.

3. FOCUS ON TEMPERATURE

Cooking is about time and temperature, so it's important to understand how to observe your smoker. You'll struggle to maintain temperatures if you think smoke needs to roll from the pit throughout the entire cooking time. If you add wood to the fire every time the smoke begins to die down, you'll end up with a lot of ash building up in the fire pan, erratic temperatures, and a sense of frustration. While smoke is an important component of this type of cooking, it should never be used as a primary means of knowing how well cooking is going, or your smoker is working.

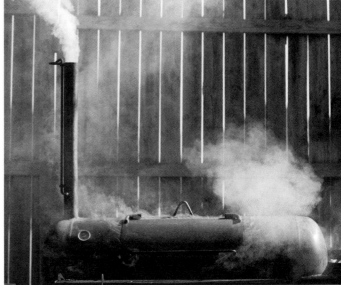

2. BUILD THE RIGHT FIRE

Building a fire that's too small or too large is part of learning how an individual pit behaves. Longer cooking times, such as for large cuts of red meat, will require a bigger bed of coals to maintain heat over many hours. Shorter cooking times, such as for smaller pieces of delicate meats, fish, or vegetables, require shorter periods of smoking but still depend on heat from the coals. Longer cooks should need bigger fires; however, a well-insulated cooking chamber and firebox will reduce your need for fuel.

   Whatever you're smoking, never assume you'll build the same fire for every occasion. Carefully consider what you're cooking and what outside factors (weather, quality of the wood, and so on) may affect the process, and adjust accordingly. The more you smoke, the more you'll learn how to tweak the fire and get your pit to the temperatures you need on a consistent basis.

4. BE PATIENT

Opening the smoker too often, or constantly tinkering with the smoker and meats, can lead to disappointing results, so trust the process and don't rush it. I joke with beginners that nobody ever said "I have an hour… let's smoke some meat!" Be aware that this will take time, so plan ahead and enjoy the process and artistry of crafting carefully prepared food. The rewards are well worth it.

THE SMOKERS

Choosing a smoker is a critical component for successful smoking. Other factors – such as cost, size, and heat control – will help you pick the best smoker for you and your needs. Here, I cover both the popular offset and upright smokers, as well as other options.

OFFSET SMOKERS

In an offset smoker, the firebox is separate from the cooking chamber, allowing rising hot air and smoke that's generated in the firebox to circulate into the cooking chamber and cook the meat indirectly. It has either a simple hole opening between the firebox and the cooking chamber or a vent-controlled opening that allows more precise control of air flow to better hit target temperatures.

> **Because hot air will rise at a rapid rate, closing the flue on the opening is one way to restrict air flow and keep temperatures down.**

❶ Vent (inflow)
❷ Firebox
❸ Water pan
❹ Cooking chamber
❺ Cooking grate
❻ Vent stack (outflow)

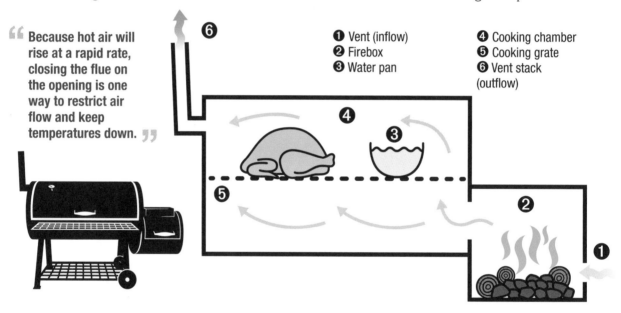

PROS

SMOKE:
Smoke generated is higher and better in amount and quality.

FLAVOUR:
Because these smokers depend on real wood fires for smoke, the flavours imparted are more pronounced.

SIMPLICITY:
Their straightforward design and minimal features make them ideal for smoking enthusiasts.

CONS

SIZE:
Their horizontal design means they can take up a lot of space.

TIME AND ATTENTION:
They require more focus during the smoking process. You have to build the fire by hand, and cooking times can be longer.

COST AND QUALITY:
Inexpensive offset pits can often be built from very thin metal which is inefficient in holding heat.

UPRIGHT SMOKERS

Upright smokers (also known as "water" or "bullet" smokers) use a more vertical design to cook food indirectly. The firebox is directly below the cooking chamber, diverting smoke and heat around a central water pan or plate that serves as a heat barrier and a source of moisture, allowing smoke to rise into the cooking chamber.

A WATER PAN HELPS CREATE MOIST HEAT, WHICH ACTUALLY COOKS FOOD MORE QUICKLY THAN INDIRECT, DRY HEAT.

" Upright smokers that use water pans do a good job of maintaining low temperatures over long cooking times, due to how stable water remains once it boils at 100°C (212°F). "

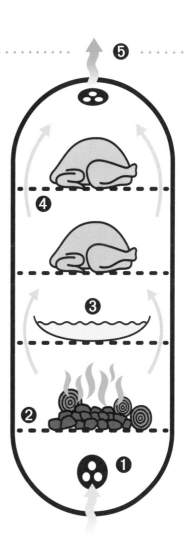

❶ Vent (inflow)
❷ Fire grate
❸ Water pan
❹ Cooking grate
❺ Vent (outflow)

PROS

TIME:
Because of their smaller size compared to other smokers, cooking times are often shorter.

TEMPERATURE:
The water pan retains heat from the fire and keeps the cooking chamber temperature fairly stable.

SIZE:
Most upright smokers are relatively compact.

CONS

MOISTURE:
Their higher moisture levels mean attaining a high-quality "bark" around the outside of meat can prove difficult.

COST AND QUALITY:
As with offset smokers, they can vary wildly based on size, quality of materials, and design.

LIMIT ON LARGER CUTS:
The compact nature of these smokers can limit the size of the cuts of meat you can cook in them.

CABINET SMOKERS

Cabinet smokers are often charcoal-fuelled units and follow a design similar to that of upright smokers. However, they differ from regular upright models because they focus more on insulation and heat-retaining properties than on air flow and firebox capacity.

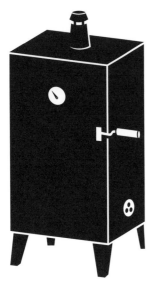

❶ Vent (inflow)
❷ Firebox
❸ Water pan
❹ Cooking grate
❺ Vent stack (outflow)

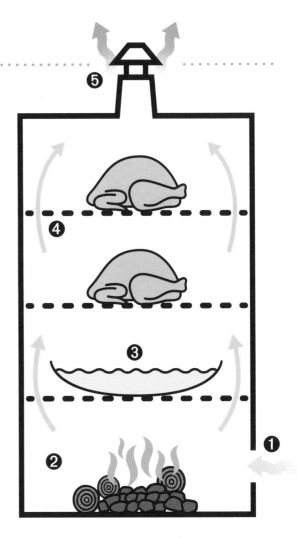

❝ Cabinet smokers use double walls of steel that contain various types of heat-resistant insulation. ❞

PROS

INSULATION:
Because cabinet smokers are built to emphasize insulating properties, quality cabinet smokers usually hold heat well.

SIZE:
Because of their vertical design, cabinet smokers will often fit into smaller locations and take up less space than more horizontal designs.

EASY ACCESS:
The design allows easy access to what you are cooking, and to the firebox in case you need to add more wood.

CONS

CAPACITY:
While some can be fitted with larger water- and fuel-holding pans for longer cooking times, most aren't ideal.

COST:
Often expensive and not as versatile as other smokers when you need multiple temperature zones for different meats cooked together, but can be an investment with a few extras.

MOISTURE:
Their higher moisture levels mean attaining a high-quality "bark" around the outside of meat can prove difficult.

ELECTRIC SMOKERS

Electric smokers have become more popular, because you can set them to a specific temperature and not have to worry about heat spikes and drops, just as with a conventional oven. The controls also mirror those for electric ovens, complete with timer functions and food temperature probe options.

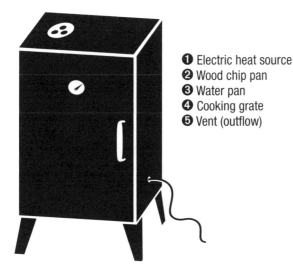

❶ Electric heat source
❷ Wood chip pan
❸ Water pan
❹ Cooking grate
❺ Vent (outflow)

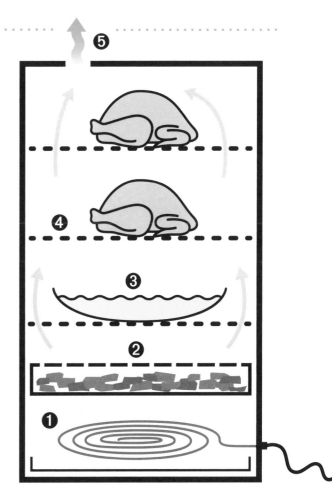

> Electric smokers are the easiest to set and maintain at low temperatures because their electric coils won't fluctuate with the outside elements, such as wind. "

PROS

CONTROL:
Electric coils provide the heat source, offering consistency when building and maintaining temperature.

CONVENIENCE:
Precise temperature controls help you maintain a steady temperature, which means it requires less attention.

STORAGE:
Electric smokers usually have small footprints, making space concerns minimal. Also, because they use only a small amount of wood chips, storing fuel is easy.

CONS

FLAVOUR:
Because a small amount of wood chips produce the smoke, the smoke flavour is mild.

SMOKE:
Capturing a distinct smoke ring in meats is difficult to achieve because of the small amount of smouldering wood.

AIR FLOW:
Because no actual fire exists, air flow controls are minimal, making the cooking passive. The warm air moves across the foods at a slow pace.

CHARCOAL GRILL SMOKING

While you may not think it's possible to smoke on a charcoal grill, with a little creativity, it can work well as a smoker. Because they're not well insulated, they're less ideal for longer cooking times and larger cuts. However, they can work well for meats that need shorter cooking times.

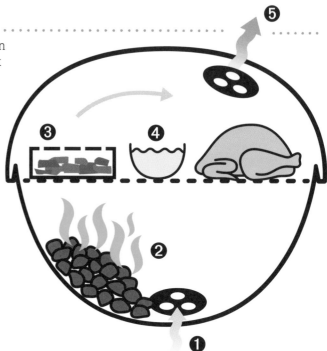

❶ Vent (inflow)
❷ "Banked" charcoal
❸ Wood chip box
❹ Water pan
❺ Vent (outflow)

To set up your charcoal grill for smoking:

1 Put the coals in a compact pile in your grill and then start your fire.

2 After the coals begin to glow, use a small shovel or another heat-resistant tool to bank the coals to one side of the grill basin.

3 Place the cooking grate over the coals, orienting the opening in the grate above the coals. If your grate doesn't have an opening in it, you'll need to add more charcoal before placing the meat onto the cooking grate.

4 Place an aluminum pan filled with water and a chip box or a perforated foil packet filled with wood chips on the cooking grate directly above the coals.

5 Place your food on the grill grate opposite the water pan, being sure to orient the fatter, bulkier end of the meat toward the coals to ensure it doesn't dry out.

❝ **Trying to cook larger cuts, such as brisket or pork shoulder, is very hard on a charcoal grill. However, smaller cuts – such as ribs, chicken, turkey, or fish – are much more manageable to smoke on a charcoal grill. ❞**

WHAT TO KNOW
• The area above the coals is the direct-heat cooking zone, while the area on the opposite side is the indirect-heat cooking zone.
• While smoking on a charcoal grill has its limitations, it allows you some control over your fire, as you can easily add or subtract fuel.
• Add enough charcoal to fill one side of the smoker, while making sure the charcoal doesn't cover the air vent on the bottom of the grill.

GAS GRILL SMOKING

Gas grills are a little easier to manage than charcoal grills when it comes to creating indirect cooking zones. Grills that have multiple gas burners below the cooking grate also have temperature controls you can adjust as needed.

❶ Heat source (burner)
❷ Ceramic briquettes or lava rock
❸ Wood chip box
❹ Water pan

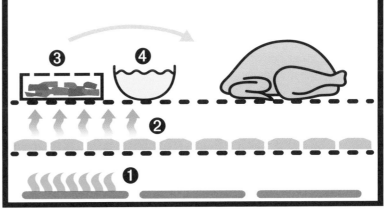

To set up your gas grill for smoking:

1 Determine where your indirect cooking zone will be located, and light the burners opposite the cooking zone (you should always light fewer than half of the burners).

2 Place an aluminium pan filled with water on the cooking grate, directly over the lit burners. (The water creates a heat barrier between the gas burners and the meat to be smoked.)

3 Place a chip box or a perforated foil packet filled with wood chips on the cooking grate directly above the coals and next to the water pan.

4 Place your food on the grill grate opposite the water pan, being sure to orient the fatter, bulkier end of the meat toward the heat source.

❝ **I've been astonished by several of my friends' ability to cook small briskets on gas grills set up in this way. While I was sceptical at first, the proof was in the eating. The smoke flavour wasn't as intense or as deeply infused into the meat as it would be on a traditional smoker; however, the fat rendered well, and the bark that formed was a pleasant surprise.** ❞

WHAT TO KNOW
• A downside to gas grill smoking is the lack of burning wood or charcoal, so you have less control over your fire as well as less smoke.
• Because gas grills can heat up quickly, with no vents to allow heat to escape, watch the grill closely to ensure your protein doesn't overcook.
• Light fewer than half the burners on the grill, as more will probably create direct-heat cooking, so your food will be cooked before it's had a chance to absorb the smoke flavours.

THE ELEMENTS of SMOKING

Smoking is an indirect cooking process that depends on several distinct elements to achieve perfect meats and other foods. And, because every component of the process is directly related to the others, they're all equally important.

TIME

Unlike grilling over a regular barbecue, smoking is a long process that requires time and patience. However, the longer cooking times allow the smoke flavours to become infused in the meats and – as with a slow cooker – to allow tough, fatty cuts of meat to become tender and delicious.

Compare the different cooking methods for grilling a 450g (1lb) ribeye steak:

• **Direct heat:** The steak is cooked for 4 minutes per side, with a 10-minute rest period, to achieve an internal temperature of 57–60°C (135–140°F).

• **Indirect heat with a reverse sear:** The steak is smoked for 35–40 minutes using indirect heat to achieve an internal temperature of 57–60°C (135–140°F). It is then seared directly on the coals, or in a cast-iron pan, for 2 minutes per side, and finally has a 10-minute rest period.

BE PATIENT
While this book contains many recipes that require cooking times of less than 1 hour, you must have patience during the smoking process, or else you'll become frustrated with low-quality results. The best cooks don't talk in terms of "*x* minutes until something's done". Instead, they measure time in hours and never try to rush the process… or the food.

ENJOY THE PROCESS
One of the greatest challenges for cooks is learning how to fine-tune their smoker for lengthy cooking times at low temperatures. However, this tinkering with different combinations of coal and wood, and finding solutions that work, is one of the pleasures of smoking meats; you'll gain a sense of real accomplishment when you achieve that perfect balance.

TEMPERATURE

There are many factors that can impact the level of control you'll have as you learn to smoke food. Outside elements – including but not limited to wind, cold weather, and the fuel wood's relative dryness – can all compete to either increase or reduce temperatures during cooking.

Some smokers work best with large fires that are controlled by the draw of the chimney and restricted air flow through the various vents in the cooking chamber and firebox. Others require smaller fires and fewer hot coals, as well as different combinations of draw and vent control.

As a general rule, smokers are designed to cook from temperatures as low as 82°C (180°F) to as high as 149°C (300°F), or even higher in some cases. However, indirect cooking usually works best in the range of 121–135°C (250–275°F). Whatever you're cooking, though, you'll want to maintain even cooking temperatures throughout the smoking process.

CLEAN SMOKER = GOOD AIR FLOW
Maintaining a clean smoker – including keeping the amount of ash build-up in the firebox, and the amount of build-up on the cooking grates, to a minimum – should always be a priority. As well as being good basic hygiene, by cleaning well you'll ensure you're not restricting air flow due to build-up from previous smokes.

" Use a wire brush with stout bristles to clean the grates. Never use oven cleaner or other harsh chemicals when cleaning any cooking surfaces. "

AIR FLOW

How much air you expose your fire to directly determines how hot it will burn and how quickly it will ignite and consume fuel. For instance, restricting the air flowing into the firebox by closing the vents will cause the fire to burn at a lower temperature. Conversely, allowing too much air flow into the firebox may cause the fire to burn too hot and your fuel to burn too quickly. It may also result in temperature spikes in the cooking chamber.

Typically, after lighting the fire, all vents on a smoker are opened for maximum air flow. This brings the cooking chamber's temperature up to the target much more quickly. The air flow is then adjusted throughout the cooking process by restricting, or maximizing, the air flow using various combinations of the chimney flue and the firebox vents.

Because air flow is key to properly smoked food, don't forget to check your smoker for potential problems. For instance, if your food isn't smoking as well as it once did, you might have a leak in a vent or another internal issue.

INSULATION

A high-quality, well-insulated firebox and cooking chamber on a smoker are much easier to manage throughout the cooking process than those on cheaper smokers built using thin walls of rolled steel. Reaching the target cooking temperatures and maintaining them for hours and hours can be fairly easy with a well-insulated pit.

The rule when it comes to insulation is that the amount you spend on the smoker will directly correlate to how well insulated it is, as well as how well it holds heat. While inexpensive, non-insulated smokers may work just fine for items with short cooking times, such as fish or smaller cuts of chicken, they are difficult to manage over medium to long cooking projects that need 5 hours or more.

Look for smokers that are built with heavy, 5mm (¼in) thick steel; this will ensure your smoker holds heat well. If you buy a cheaper model made with thin, rolled steel, you're going to have a harder time keeping it at the correct temperature. However, if you're stuck with a cheaper smoker that can't hold heat for long cooking times, there are things you can do to help. Try wrapping the cooking chamber with a fire-resistant welding blanket to help retain heat. This is also a handy trick to use when smoking in colder weather.

SMOKING IN INCLEMENT WEATHER
If you're one of those people who enjoys smoking during the winter or even during rain storms, you can find many products online that will allow you to protect the outside of your smoker from the elements, such as high-heat-resistant fibreglass and ceramic blankets. These products will also help you build and maintain your fires to ensure you have the necessary internal temperatures in your smoker to smoke your favourite meats and other foods.

STARTERS, FUEL, and WOOD

Making the best fuel and wood choices for what you're trying to achieve is a vital component of a successful smoking process.

CHOOSING THE FUEL

What is the best fuel for starting the fire?

Natural hardwood lump charcoal is the easiest and cleanest method for fuelling a fire. It produces much less ash than briquettes, keeping more air circulating under and around the fire, and producing a cleaner smoke that won't taint your food with chemical compounds.

Is it okay to use cheaper charcoal briquettes?

Some charcoal briquette brands contain chemical additives that might aid in combustion but also impart unnatural flavours to food. It's therefore best to avoid the cheap stuff and instead use only natural hardwood lump charcoal from a good supplier.

HOW MUCH CHARCOAL WILL YOU NEED TO START THE FIRE?
The amount of charcoal required is roughly equivalent to one-third of the firebox or fire grate capacity. The goal is to always have enough charcoal to ignite your cooking wood and produce even and steady heat for the duration of cooking.

STARTING THE FIRE

What's the best way to start a fire?

What you use to start your fire will impart flavour to whatever you put on your pit. Therefore, while you can always use a stick lighter or common kitchen or stick matches to start your fire, I prefer a hand-held propane torch, which is a much more intense source of heat and starts a fire much faster than matches or lighters. You can also use an electric coil grill starter.

Is it okay to use lighter fluid to start fires?

You should never use lighter fluid to start your fires. It contains toxic chemicals that can be transferred to your food. Additionally, lighter fluid is extremely flammable and can create vapours that erupt when allowed to build up in a firebox prior to a fire being lit.

CHOOSING THE WOOD

What size wood should you use?
This depends on your firebox's capacity and the type of smoker you're using. From wood chips and chunks to 55–60cm (22–24in) logs, many sizes are possible.

> **CAUTION!**
> Always avoid woods from coniferous trees, such as pine or spruce, which contain compounds that can make you sick. Also, never smoke with any wood that has been treated, painted, or stained in any way.

How long should cooking wood be seasoned?
Logs split and dried for 9–12 months burn clean and hot. Because wood seasoned for a shorter time will produce less heat and emit heavier, less clean smoke, it's important to ask your supplier how long the wood has been seasoned.

How can you tell if wood is properly seasoned?
Well-seasoned wood should be cracked on the ends and should not feel disproportionately heavy for its size. If it hasn't been properly seasoned, it will burn at a lower temperature and produce a less desirable type of smoke.

HOW MUCH WOOD WILL YOU NEED?
This will depend on a variety of factors, including the type of smoker you're using, how well your smoker is insulated, the length of cooking time a recipe requires, and the quality of air flow and fire you're able to produce. You also need to bear in mind environmental factors, such as the outdoor temperature. Because of these varying factors, each recipe in this book lists a general range of amounts you should have on hand for each smoking project.

SPLIT LOGS
These offer the longest-burning source of smoke and flavour. Split logs are best for larger smoker types, such as offset smokers.

High	7–10+ logs
Medium	5–7 logs
Low	3–5 logs

WOOD CHUNKS
A more versatile option, wood chunks provide steady smoke and flavour for long periods of time. These are ideal for cabinet or offset smokers.

High	4–6 bags
Medium	2–4 bags
Low	1–2 bags

WOOD CHIPS
While they impart great flavour, you may need to soak them to prevent them from burning up too quickly. Wood chips work best in upright smokers.

High	not recommended
Medium	3–5 bags
Low	1–3 bags

BUILDING and FINE-TUNING the FIRE

Without a good fire, your wood won't produce adequate smoke, your pit won't achieve proper temperature, and your food won't cook properly. So building and fine-tuning a good fire in your pit is the first crucial step for successful smoking.

BUILDING THE FIRE

1 Clean any ash remnants out of the firebox by using a shovel or another appropriate tool.

2 Fill the firebox grate with all-natural hardwood lump charcoal. A good gauge for the amount to use is roughly one-third the capacity of the firebox grate space.

3 Light the charcoal with a hand-held propane torch. A propane torch will provide intense, direct heat and will work better than matches or stick lighters. An electric coil starter is another good option for quickly and cleanly starting a fire. (Don't use chemical fire starters or lighter fluid to start your fire.)

4 Be patient and let the fire die down until your coals are glowing orange and releasing significant heat (about 15 minutes). Once the fire has died down and the coals are glowing orange, use a shovel to spread them evenly across the surface of the firebox grate.

FIRE BUILDING TIPS

• **Use the right amounts of fuel and wood.** Building too small a fire and having to add wood to maintain an even temperature will create heat spikes and troughs that can cause your meats to become tougher than anticipated and to take longer to cook.

• **Don't worry about the smoke.** Don't be concerned with the amount of smoke coming from the pit. You'll have periods of heavy smoke initially, but after 25 minutes, the wood chunks stop producing heavy smoke and begin to break down into coals. This is a good thing, because coals produce even heat over a longer period of time.

• **For longer cooks, add wood in stages.** If your cooking time requires you to add wood to maintain the required temperature, add smaller amounts at a time. Put in just 1–2 pieces each time your temperature starts to drop by a few degrees. How well insulated your smoker is will determine the frequency at which you'll need to add wood to maintain a steady temperature. Remember, cooking is achieved by low, even heat, not smoke.

5 Add your cooking wood; seasoned wood will smoulder and ignite on the hot charcoal fairly rapidly. I usually add 3–4 wood pieces initially because it's easier to knock the temperature down in an offset pit by using the vents and damper.

TROUBLESHOOTING

As you discover the personality of your pit, you'll develop a sharper sense of what you need to do to fine-tune your fire and achieve the right temperature. While learning how your pit behaves can be a labour of love, here are tips to help you along.

SOLUTIONS FOR COMMON PIT PROBLEMS

1. What if the smoke coming from the pit is very dark (almost black)?
The fire is dampered too low and is causing the wood to smoulder at too low a temperature. I recommend opening all the vents as well as the chimney and thus allowing the wood to burn at a higher temperature.

2. Is it possible to oversmoke meats?
Smoke flavour is a matter of personal preference, so it's really down to your own taste. However, if you feel your pit is causing your meat to taste bitter or acrid, your pit might be dirty. There's also a possibility that the wood you're using is too green and giving off too heavy a smoke. So use seasoned wood and ensure your pit grates are clean.

3. What if my pit isn't holding an even temperature?
Check that your vents are clear and that ash build-up in the firebox hasn't caused your fire to smoulder. Sometimes, stirring the coals will raise the temperature back up, because when ash is dispersed, more oxygen can reach the coals.

4. What if my pit runs too hot?
Be sure that all the vents are nearly fully closed and that the chimney isn't drawing too much hot air away from the firebox and through the cooking chamber. The first place to check is the firebox vent, and the second is the chimney vent. Restricting the draw may solve this problem all by itself.

Keeping your firebox clear of ash and debris will keep the pit working at peak performance.

Because proper air flow is a common cause of pit problems, keep vents clear of debris and obstructions, both inside and outside the pit.

If your meats are overcooking on one side, place a sheet of foil between the heat source and the food to create a more evenly balanced cooking environment.

5. My pit temperature is correct, but my meats are overcooked in places, or burned. What can I do to minimize this?

Point the smallest ends of your meats away from the heat source and not too close to the fire. You can also use a sheet of foil as a heat shield so direct heat doesn't reach your food.

6. What if I can't get my pit up to the required temperature?

Be sure the vents to the firebox are open and that air flow isn't restricted by ash or debris. Reconsider the amount of charcoal used to start the fire, or the amount of cooking wood that was initially added. Sometimes, pits need more fuel to get to the required temperature, such as during cold-weather months, or if the wood isn't fully seasoned.

7. Is the water pan in a vertical or cabinet smoker always necessary?

I recommend using the water pan as a way to maintain even temperature in the pit. The heat the water holds gives some protection from variations in the fire, such as flare-ups. However, if you're seeking higher temperatures during shorter cooking times, you can ditch the water pan.

8. How often do I need to tend the fire?

During a longer cooking time (4 or more hours), it's a good rule of thumb to tend the fire once every hour. Either add more fuel or stir the coals to maintain an even cooking temperature.

DON'T RUSH THE PROCESS
Hastily preparing or neglecting the fire and pit temperature will damage your desired overall outcome. Consider smoking as a blend of technique and artistry. Give yourself time to learn your pit, and be patient with longer cooking times. This will help you become a master at imparting new flavours into the foods you smoke.

SEASONING and FLAVOURING

Three things combine to help you achieve great taste: purchasing high-quality meats, seasoning with dry rubs or brines, and basting or saucing during smoking. Together, these elements will help bring out your food's hidden flavours.

SEASONING

When it comes to smoking, you prepare the food by applying seasonings, and resting or brining the meat for as long as 10 hours before smoking. These steps create deep, rich flavours that – along with the wood smoke – often allow a finished product to stand on its own.

Seasoning with rubs

Food should retain its natural flavours after smoking. Dry rubs or simple treatments of salt and pepper, or brown or granulated sugar, will help enhance those natural flavours, not mask them. However, don't be afraid to add other ingredients to basic rub recipes as a fun and creative way to personalize your recipes.

Resting

Chilled foods will contract and tense up if they're placed directly into the pit. Resting meat at room temperature allows the muscle fibres to relax and feel natural to the touch. Additionally, resting allows seasonings to be drawn into the muscle fibres and to season the meat more deeply.

Brining

Submerging poultry in a salt water solution is similar to the dry rub process: salt is drawn into the muscle fibres and seasons the meat while also drawing in moisture. Brining can infuse a wide range of flavours, but will also cause the foods to "sweat" more during the cooking process.

Dry rubs and seasonings should be applied to the surfaces and crevices of meat using a rubbing or patting motion.

Resting is an important step in seasoning. It may be done in a few minutes or, if a deeper level of seasoning is desired, overnight.

FLAVOURING

Flavouring with wood

Each type of wood carries a different aroma and flavour that will deeply season the items in the pit. Larger cuts such as brisket can become overly smoked if robust cooking woods (such as mesquite) are used throughout the long cooking time, so choose a milder wood such as oak for these longer cooks. More delicate items with faster cooking times, such as fish and shellfish, will take on the milder flavours of a wood such as oak nicely. For medium cooking times for items such as chicken or ribs, use hickory or pecan that won't overwhelm.

Basting and saucing

Throughout the cooking time, a thin layer of a basting mixture is dabbed onto the meats to create a layer of flavour that will meld with the smoke and seasonings. These mixtures should be low in sugar, to prevent burning during long cooking times, and work best when applied toward the final one-third of the cook time.

Saucing is more about flavouring. Sauces are usually higher in sugar content than basting mixtures, so they're generally applied at the end of cooking time to avoid burning.

CHOOSING THE FLAVOUR

While there are many types of wood you can use to impart unique flavours and levels of smoke to your food, here are some of my favourites.

TYPE	SMOKE	BEST USE
Apple	Mild, with a fruity flavour	Poultry and pork
Cherry	Mild, sweet, and fruity	Poultry and beef
Mesquite	Strong and highly aromatic	Heavier meats, such as beef, lamb, and game
Pecan	Sweet and mild, similar to hickory	Poultry, beef, and pork
Oak	Mild to heavy	Beef, pork, fish, and shellfish

DIPPING
Dipping is similar to saucing but involves foods being dunked in a sauce after being removed from the smoker. There is some confusion between the terms sauce and dip, but they are different.

Sauces should be applied towards the end of the cooking process with a nylon-bristled brush.

TOOLS of the TRADE

No matter what kind of smoker you use or what foods you're smoking, you'll want to have some essential basic tools on hand, and also consider some other nice-to-have gadgets that will help make the process easier.

ESSENTIAL TOOLS

Instant-read thermometer:
An instant-read thermometer is used to gauge the internal temperature of meats. Whether you use a digital or dial thermometer, make sure to calibrate it before each cook.

Kitchen shears:
A good pair of kitchen shears can make many tasks easier, including cutting herbs, cutting through tough connective tissue, opening bottles, and cracking lobster claws. Look for shears that are sharp and made from high-quality stainless steel.

Basting brushes and mops:
Buy brushes with synthetic bristles that can go into your dishwasher, and thoroughly wash them after each use. Also, inexpensive paintbrushes are a cheaper option than basting brushes and work equally well; plus, you won't have to worry about ruining them by forgetting to wash them right away.

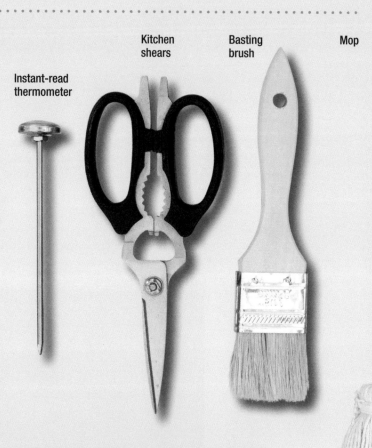

Instant-read thermometer

Kitchen shears

Basting brush

Mop

BUY THE BEST TOOLS YOU CAN AFFORD
Because using your smoker can become such an everyday hobby, you should make an investment in your tools. You'll want durable products you won't have to replace every summer, and you'll want to know that whatever tool you're using won't fail you at a critical moment, potentially ruining food, or causing injury. Paying a little more now will mean spending less over the long term.

Heavy-duty tongs

Heavy-duty tongs:

Reaching into the smoker with bare hands is not only uncomfortable but also dangerous. Protect yourself with a pair of long, heavy-duty tongs that fit your grip and you'll always feel confident and safe as you lift heavier cuts of meat.

BECAUSE THESE TOOLS ARE CRITICAL TO SMOKING, MAKE SURE TO KEEP THEM CLEAN. IT ALSO NEVER HURTS TO HAVE MORE THAN ONE HANDY, IN CASE SOMETHING HAPPENS TO YOUR FIRST.

NICE-TO-HAVE TOOLS

Coal and ash shovel:

Although most shovels will work, a flat coal and ash shovel makes removing ash from the firebox quick and easy, and it eliminates any safety concerns about residual heat.

Ash bucket:

Use a galvanized bucket to collect ash you've cleaned from the firebox. This allows you to dispense with any worry about ash being cool enough to dispose of immediately. Try to find a bucket that is the right height to sit just below the firebox doors.

Meat spike:

Use a long steel meat spike to move meats on the smoker. Not only can you move them around the smoker quickly, but you can also gauge doneness when the spike goes into each piece. While you can have a spike custom made, or buy one online, you can also find items in a hardware store that will work well.

Propane blowtorch:

Although it's not essential, a propane blowtorch is good to have on hand for starting your fires quickly and efficiently. It produces a much more intense source of heat than ordinary stick matches or stick lighters.

Blowtorch

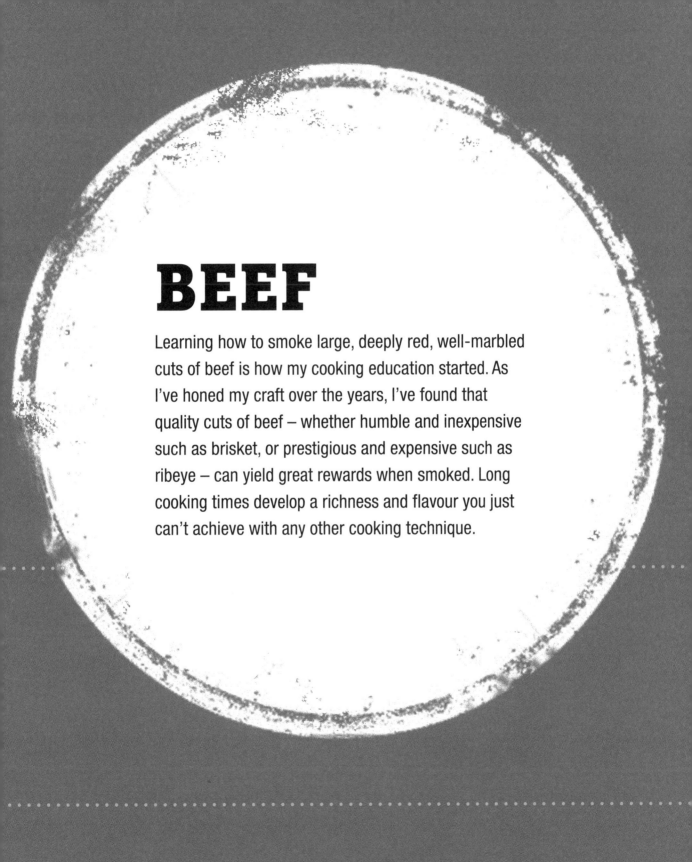

BEEF

Learning how to smoke large, deeply red, well-marbled cuts of beef is how my cooking education started. As I've honed my craft over the years, I've found that quality cuts of beef – whether humble and inexpensive such as brisket, or prestigious and expensive such as ribeye – can yield great rewards when smoked. Long cooking times develop a richness and flavour you just can't achieve with any other cooking technique.

SMOKING BEEF: WHAT YOU NEED to KNOW

Smoking beef is all about slow cooking, and developing that crusty outer bark, and because beef has a high fat content and large amounts of connective tissue, it often requires longer cooking times, so you will need patience. Follow these tips and you'll find yourself successfully smoking beautiful cuts of beef in no time.

IN THE KITCHEN

Learn about beef before you smoke
If you're new to smoking beef, research fat marbling, what you can do with different cuts, and even how to butcher your own cuts.

Fresh beef will offer tastier results
Frozen beef is often cheaper than fresh. Some cooks say frozen is also more tender and that fresh beef starts to age too quickly. But, as with any meat, the proof is in the eating.

Keep your seasonings simple
To ensure you don't overseason the meat, start by simply seasoning beef cuts with salt and pepper, and do a few test cooks to find what your ideal seasoning profile is before the smoke component is added. Some people prefer a heavy hand with the seasoning, while others prefer a more minimalist approach, but it's important not to overdo it until you know what you like, and how the wood will impact those choices.

PURCHASE QUALITY CUTS
Cuts of beef need to be purchased with care

SOURCE	SMOKE QUALITY	DESCRIPTION
Organic grass-fed	Excellent	This comes from well-raised and well-hung cattle and has significant marbling. It is the best beef you can buy and is excellent for smoking.
Dry-hung	Good	While this is a more affordable and appealing alternative to organic grass-fed, make sure it has enough fat marbling throughout.
"Aged"	Poor	This usually has less marbling than organic grass-fed or dry-hung, which means it's leaner and prone to becoming dry. It's also usually wet-aged, which can inhibit the quality of the "bark".
Standard supermarket	Poor	This won't be marbled and will have been wet-aged. It probably won't be worthwhile to smoke, or to eat in large quantities however prepared.
Supermarket economy	Poor	Avoid this because it might be from older cattle, have no marbling, and can be imported from countries with lower welfare standards.

Learn to balance flavours

One skill to master in smoking beef is how to pair rubs or sauces with the meat you're smoking and the wood you're using. You don't want one to overpower or undermine another element. Instead, you want them to work together to create moist, flavoursome, and well-received dishes that will have people clamouring for seconds and thirds.

Get creative with leftovers

Smoked beef cuts should be served immediately after the required resting period. However, if you find you have leftovers from larger cuts, pack them in zip-lock plastic bags and place them in the refrigerator for up to 1 week, or the freezer for up to 6 months. Leftover smoked beef is a fantastic addition to other recipes.

LOOK CAREFULLY AT PACKAGING. SADLY, STORES OFTEN CONFUSE SHOPPERS WITH AMBIGUOUS WORDING.

ON THE SMOKER

Being armed with some basic knowledge around the smoker will increase your odds for successfully smoking beef.

Start small when first considering which cuts to smoke

Start your beef-smoking experience with a brisket in the 2.7–4kg (6–8lb) range, or a rack of short ribs. These cuts are forgiving because they cook evenly, have adequate fat for protection from heat, and are easy to check for temperature.

Experiment with wood choices

Using oak to smoke beef ensures you have a hardy wood that will keep your smoker temperature consistent. But once you have more experience, don't limit yourself to oak; other woods, such as mesquite and pecan, can impart wonderful flavours to any beef cut.

Watch smoker temps and cook times

Maintaining the fire and keeping the smoker's temperature consistent throughout cooking will result in more uniform cooking and better-tasting dishes. Don't be afraid to experiment with smoking, but be cautious when you're pushing the limits.

Develop a sense about how well-cooked meat looks and feels

As you smoke beef, pay attention to how the bark forms on the outside of large cuts, and test the fattiest areas for their firmness, or amount of jiggle. In time, you won't need an instant-read thermometer and will gauge doneness by a simple poke with your finger or with heavy-duty tongs.

Consider the final smoking stages

Although many accomplished smoker cooks choose to wrap their cuts in butcher paper or foil to hold in moisture during the final cooking stage, I prefer not to do so. A brisket, shoulder, or beef rib joint that's wrapped in butcher paper will steam within the wrapping, which can then diminish the quality of the bark. While the resting period can help the bark firm back up, I feel it is best when the cut is not wrapped.

Don't skip the rest

Resting beef allows for residual cooking and for the juices to return to their rightful place within the cuts. A cut carved too early will dry out quickly and the juices will be left on the cutting board rather than mopped up from a plate.

BEEF CUTS

Understanding where cuts come from on a cow, how they're used, and how well they'll take smoke will help you make the right choices when deciding what you want to cook.

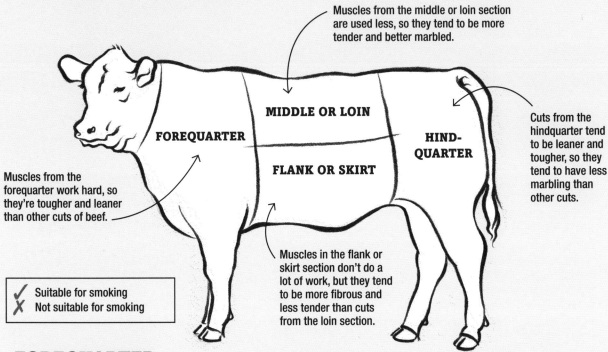

Muscles from the middle or loin section are used less, so they tend to be more tender and better marbled.

MIDDLE OR LOIN

FOREQUARTER

FLANK OR SKIRT

HIND-QUARTER

Cuts from the hindquarter tend to be leaner and tougher, so they tend to have less marbling than other cuts.

Muscles from the forequarter work hard, so they're tougher and leaner than other cuts of beef.

Muscles in the flank or skirt section don't do a lot of work, but they tend to be more fibrous and less tender than cuts from the loin section.

✓ Suitable for smoking
✗ Not suitable for smoking

FOREQUARTER

Chuck or shoulder

Short ribs

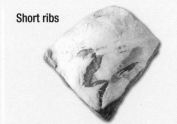

Brisket

✓ **Chuck or shoulder area:** This contains bone-in chuck steaks and roasts (such as round blade), as well as boneless clod.

✗ **Foreshin:** These provide tough meat that's primarily used for stews and soups, as it needs long cooking. The foreshank is smokeable.

✓ **Rib:** This contains part of the short ribs (sometimes called Jacob's ladder), which is an excellent candidates for smoking.

✓ **Plate:** This is the other source for short ribs, as well as the outside skirt steak that's trimmed from the face of the ribs.

✓ **Brisket:** Often used for smoking but also cured to make pastrami and salt beef, brisket is sometimes trimmed into 'flat' and 'point' sections, terms which describe its shape. Brisket is excellent smoked, and can be served in a number of ways, including sliced or pulled.

MIDDLE OR LOIN

Fillet

Ribeye

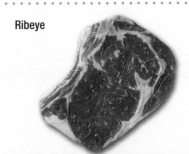

✓ **Beef fillet:** Taken from just below the ribs and along the central vertebrae, this is certainly the most expensive cut from the carcass. Fillet smokes beautifully and yields richly flavoured, tender meat.

✓ **Fore rib of beef, Chateaubriand, Wing rib, and bone-in Sirloin:** All these roasts come from the centre portion of the cow and all of them yield good meat for smoking. Just remember to keep the fat in place so the cuts don't dry out in the smoker, but still remain flavoursome.

✓ **Ribeye roast and steaks:** These are some of the most sought-after cuts because of their higher fat content and tenderness.

✓ **T-bone steaks:** These are identified by their distinct T-shaped bone. They are very similar to porterhouse steaks, but include a smaller portion of the fillet.

✓ **Porterhouse steaks:** Many believe these to be the most flavoursome steaks because they contain both the buttery fillet and the richly flavoured top loin.

BIGGER IS NOT BETTER
Cows offer larger cuts than other animals, but some cuts today are even bigger than they were a few decades ago. Modern farming practices have increased the size of the animal, but often welfare standards have not kept up. So don't worry about the size of your cut of beef. Instead, look for a dark ruby red colour, which indicates good dry ageing, and a marbling of creamy fat throughout. Buy from a butcher and always ask him questions; a good butcher will give you a fair amount of detail about how an animal has been raised.

FLANK OR SKIRT

✗ **Skirt steak:** This is a thin and noticeably fibrous cut that's trimmed from the diaphragm. It's a very tough and lean cut with very little marbling. Cook it in a griddle pan because it doesn't smoke well.

✗ **Flank steak:** A cut from the back portion of the belly – towards the hind leg – that is leaner than skirt steak. It's tough and fibrous and not ideal for smoking. Save this cut for flash-frying in a griddle pan.

✗ **Onglet:** Sometimes called "hanger steak" because it hangs between the ribs and the fillet. It's tender meat, but it's best cooked in a griddle pan because it tends to be more fibrous than other cuts.

HINDQUARTER

✓ **Rump roast:** Rump roasts come from the upper portion of the back of the cow and they tend to be tougher than roasts from the centre portion, but they also tend to have better marbling. You can smoke them if you watch the temperature closely and don't overcook them.

✗ **Sirloin:** This comes from an area between the loin and hindquarter of the cow. It tends to be more tender than even the rump, topside, or silverside, but the difficulty in smoking it means it should perhaps be avoided in favour of other, fattier cuts of beef.

✗ **Silverside:** Because cuts from this area are tough and quite lean, they're not marvellous for the smoking treatment.

✗ **Topside:** This cut is very lean and tough, and therefore not a good choice for smoking. Head for one of the fattier joints instead.

Meat Beef	Wood Oak	Prep time 9¼ hrs	Smoker temp 120°C (250°F)	Cook time 12–14 hrs	Rest time 1 hr	Yield Serves 14

Brisket can be a difficult cut for a cook to master, with a lot of time invested in the smoking process. But when done well, smoking brisket is worth all the trial and error.

BRISKET

THE MEAT

Large whole brisket, about 6.3kg (14lb)

• Brisket is cut from under the shoulder. Yours may be a different shape from this photograph, depending on local butchery cuts.

• Brisket should be well marbled (fat lines throughout and with broad line of fat), soft to the touch, a rich red colour, and never be frozen.

• Buy the highest-quality brisket you can afford. Higher-quality meat will have more marbling and a deeper flavour than less expensive beef.

THE FIRE

Light the pit fire 1 hour before smoking. Add wood 30 minutes before smoking.

• Target temp: 120°C (250°F)

• Wood needs: High

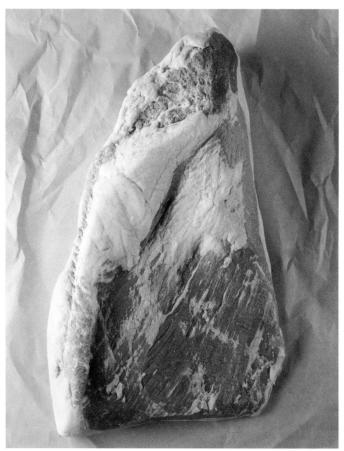

TEMPERATURE GUIDE

	Cook time	Pull temp	Serving temp
Well	12–14 hrs	77°C (170°F)	82°C (180°F)

TIME PLAN (22 HRS 50 MINS TO 24 HRS 50 MINS)

30 mins	15 mins	9 hrs	12–14 hrs	1 hr	5 mins
Build the fire	Make the rub.	Rub and rest	Smoke	Rest	Slice

✳ THE RUB

Ingredients

140g (5oz) coarse sea salt
115g (4oz) cracked black pepper
200g (7oz) granulated sugar
30g (1oz) paprika
30g (1oz) ground cumin
1 tbsp onion powder
1 tbsp garlic powder
1 tbsp cayenne pepper

❝ The salt, sugar, and paprika help to bring out the colour and flavour of the brisket, while the other spices add a little bit of heat. ❞

1 In a medium bowl, combine the salt, black pepper, sugar, paprika, cumin, onion powder, garlic powder, and cayenne pepper.

2 Apply a liberal amount of this rub to all sides of the brisket, covering the exposed meat.

3 Place the brisket in a deep tray and refrigerate, uncovered, overnight to allow the rub to deeply penetrate the meat.

4 Remove the brisket from the refrigerator and allow to rest uncovered at room temperature for at least 1 hour before going into the pit.

DON'T TRIM THE FAT CAP

The fat cap of untrimmed brisket provides insulation during cooking and forms a delicious outer bark when smoked.

Leaving the fat cap intact helps the brisket during the cooking process, protecting the beef, and creating a rich flavour and texture. Also, fat rendered during cooking is easier to remove than cold, unrendered fat.

))) THE SMOKE

1 With the pit temperature stabilized at 120°C (250°F), use tongs to place the brisket on the middle rack of the pit. Ensure the fat cap is facing up and the larger of the two ends is pointing towards the heat source.

2 Add fuel as required to maintain an even 120°C (250°F) temperature. The amount of fuel necessary will depend on weather conditions and air temperature. Don't allow the temperature to rise or fall more than 2–3°C (5–7°F) throughout the cooking process.

3 After 8 hours, insert an instant-read thermometer in the middle section of brisket to check the progress. The target temperature for removing brisket is 77°C (170°F).

4 When the brisket has reached the target temperature, in 4–6 more hours, remove it from the pit. Allow it to rest uncovered for at least 1 hour; it will continue to cook and reach the ideal serving temperature of 82°C (180°F).

5 Using a chef's knife, slice the brisket by cutting across the grain. You may find it easier to cut the brisket in half – following the natural separation lines in the muscles – before beginning to carve.

THE STALL
During the cooking time, the internal temperature of brisket stops rising, sometimes for several hours. This process is referred to as "the stall". Some scientists think it occurs because of the amount of moisture in the meat and the collagen being converted to gelatine.

This stall allows you to practice the art of barbecue patience! As long as you maintain a 120°C (250°F) temperature, your brisket will eventually move beyond this stall, and the meat temperature will rise again.

❝ It's tempting, but resist the urge to look at the brisket while it's smoking. Opening the smoker too much can cause the temperature inside to fall, so extending the cooking time. ❞

| Meat Beef | Wood Oak | Prep time 1 hr | Smoker temp 120°C (250°F) | Cook time 8–9 hrs | Rest time 45 mins | Yield Serves 4 |

Because of their size and richness, short ribs seem like an indulgence. However, despite being from a notoriously tough section of a cow, they're fairly easy to smoke.

SHORT RIBS

THE MEAT

Rack of beef short ribs 2–2.5kg (4½–5lb)

• Buy short ribs sectioned into 3-bone racks to get a piece that weighs this much. The bones will be about 20cm (8in) long.

• The large bone size helps the ribs to cook evenly, as the heat stored in the bones transfers to the meat during cooking.

• Heat trapped in the bones also means the meat carries on cooking for longer once the target internal temperature has been reached and the ribs removed from the smoker.

🔥 THE FIRE

Light the pit fire 1 hour before smoking. Add wood 30 minutes before smoking.

• Target temp: 120°C (250°F)

• Wood needs: High

TEMPERATURE GUIDE

	Cook time	Pull temp	Serving temp
Well	8–9 hrs	93°C (200°F)	96°C (205°F)

TIME PLAN (10 HRS 20 MINS TO 11 HRS 20 MINS)

30 mins	15 mins	45 mins	8–9 hrs	45 mins	5 mins
Build the fire	Make the rub	Rub and rest	Smoke	Rest	Slice

THE RUB

Ingredients

140g (5oz) coarse sea salt
115g (4oz) cracked black pepper

A RUB OF SALT AND PEPPER HELPS THE RIBS RETAIN MOISTURE AND LETS THEIR FLAVOUR SHINE.

1 Liberally season the ribs with the salt and black pepper, covering all the exposed meat.

2 Allow to rest, uncovered, at room temperature, for at least 45 minutes before going into the pit.

LONG ON MEAT AND FLAVOUR
Short ribs are certainly not short. In fact the older UK name for the cut is the lengthier sounding Jacob's Ladder (they may still be sold under that title in some places). They're taken from behind the feather blade and in front of the sirloin in a well-marbled position. This helps ensure a lot of flavour.

))) THE SMOKE

1 With the pit temperature stabilized at 120°C (250°F), use tongs to place the rib rack in the middle of the pit, meat-side up, bone-side down.

2 After 6 hours, insert an instant-read thermometer between the second and third bones to check the progress. The target temperature for removing ribs is 93°C (200°F).

3 When the ribs reach the target temperature, in 2–3 more hours, remove them from the pit. Let the meat rest uncovered for at least 45 minutes before cutting it into portions, as above.

> **If you prefer not to eat the meat from the bones, feel free to slice the meat away from the bones, cutting across the grain and portioning it.**

COMPLEMENT
THESE RIBS WITH
SWEET PICKLES OR
RED ONIONS.

44

Meat Beef	Wood Oak	Prep time 1 hr	Smoker temp 120°C (250°F)	Cook time 45 mins to 1 hr	Rest time 10 mins	Yield Serves 8

Fillet of beef is one of the most tender, expensive and sought-after cuts from a cow. While it isn't traditionally smoked as a whole cut, searing portions of the fillet after smoking creates a great smoky flavour while providing that familiar steak crust.

FILLET

THE MEAT

Fillet of beef, 1.6–1.8kg (3½–4lb), silverskin removed

• Purchase fillet with the silverskin already removed by the butcher and the fat expertly trimmed away.

• Fillets are from beneath the ribs next to the backbone and have two distinct portions: the tail end and the thick end.

THE FIRE

Light the pit fire 1 hour before smoking. Add wood 30 minutes before smoking.

• Target temp: 120°C (250°F)

• Wood needs: Low

TEMPERATURE GUIDE

	Cook time	Pull temp	Serving temp
Medium-rare	45 mins	63°C (145°F)	63°C (145°F)
Medium	1 hr	70°C (160°F)	70°C (160°F)

Thick end

Tail end

TIME PLAN (2¾–3 HRS)

30 mins	15 mins	45 mins	45 mins to 1 hr	10 mins	10 mins	10 mins
Build the fire	Make the rub	Rub and rest	Smoke	Rest	Slice and rub	Sear

✻ THE RUB

Ingredients

1 tsp coarsely ground black pepper
1½ tsp coarse sea salt
½ tsp garlic powder
½ tsp onion powder

1 In a medium bowl, thoroughly mix the coarsely ground black pepper, salt, garlic powder, and onion powder.

2 Evenly apply the rub to all surfaces of the fillet, reserving a small amount for seasoning.

3 Allow the meat to rest, uncovered, at room temperature for at least 45 minutes before going into the pit.

〗〗 THE SMOKE

1 With the pit temperature stabilized at 120°C (250°F), use tongs to place the fillet in the middle of the pit, with the thick end pointing towards the heat source.

2 After 45 minutes, insert an instant-read thermometer in the middle of the cut to check the progress. Aim for 63°C (145°F) for medium-rare meat and 70°C (160°F) for medium.

3 Remove the fillet from the pit when it reaches your preferred temperature. Allow to rest, uncovered, for 10 minutes before slicing.

ASK A BUTCHER TO HELP

Your butcher can prepare the meat for you in the right style for smoking. Ask him or her to remove the silverskin but to leave the side muscle on. While home cooks can learn to do this themselves to save a little money, it's best to have it done professionally to preserve the appearance of this attractive and valuable cut of beef.

THE TAIL AND THICK ENDS

The fillet's tail is the tapered end that begins just past the cow's ribs, while the thick end terminates toward the rear of the cow. Because the fillet does very little work, it rewards you with exceptionally tender meat and even fat marbling.

THE REVERSE SEAR
Instead of searing the meat as the initial step in the preparation – the traditional way to cook steaks – this recipe uses a hot cast-iron pan to finish the individual portions (known as a reverse sear). Depending on your cooking arrangements, you can also perform the sear on the hob in your kitchen.

SERVE SOUTHERN STYLE WITH A RICH COLESLAW AND CORNBREAD.

4 Begin heating a cast-iron pan on the barbecue, or on the hob over a high heat.

5 Portion the fillet into 8 even-sized steaks about 5cm (2in) thick and lightly season them with the reserved rub. Place the steaks in the pan and quickly sear them for 2 minutes per side. Serve immediately.

Meat Beef	**Wood** Oak	**Prep time** 1¼ hrs	**Smoker temp** 120°C (250°F)	**Cook time** 18–20 hrs	**Rest time** 1 hr	**Yield** Serves 36–40

Beef shoulder (clod) is fairly unfamiliar to even the most enthusiastic cook. But when you have time and lots of people to feed, this slow-cooking cut is definitely worth a try.

SHOULDER (CLOD)

THE MEAT

Untrimmed beef shoulder (clod), 9–10kg (18–20lb)

• Clod comes from the neck and shoulder of a cow. It has 3 muscles that vary from very tender to a little tough.

• Clod is typically more tender than brisket once cooked and can provide a more intense beef flavour than its smaller cousin.

• The large size and density of clod allows it to retain moisture even after lengthy cooking.

THE FIRE

Light the pit fire 1 hour before smoking. Add wood 30 minutes before smoking.

• Target temp: 120°C (250°F)

• Wood needs: High

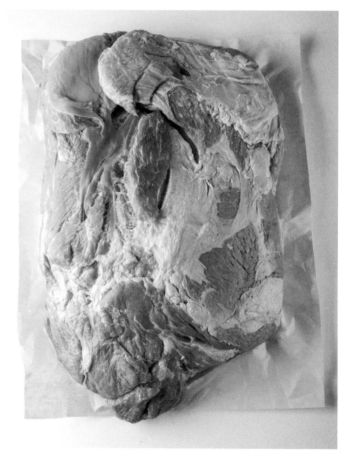

TEMPERATURE GUIDE

	Cook time	Pull temp	Serving temp
Well	18–20 hrs	79°C (175°F)	82°C (180°F)

TIME PLAN (20 HRS 55 MINS TO 22 HRS 55 MINS)

30 mins	15 mins	1 hr	18–20 hrs	1 hr	10 mins
Build the fire	Make the rub	Rub and rest	Smoke	Rest	Slice

✳ THE RUB

Ingredients

140g (5oz) coarse sea salt
115g (4oz) cracked black pepper
200g (7oz) granulated sugar
½ tsp cayenne pepper
1 tbsp ground cumin
3 tbsp garlic powder

RESTING THE CLOD OVERNIGHT ALLOWS THE FLAVOURS OF THE RUB TO INFUSE THE BEEF.

1 In a medium bowl, thoroughly mix the salt, cracked black pepper, sugar, cayenne pepper, cumin, and garlic powder.

2 Apply the rub evenly to all surfaces of the meat. Put the clod on a large tray and place, uncovered, in the refrigerator overnight.

3 Remove the meat from the refrigerator and allow to rest uncovered at room temperature for 1 hour before going into the pit.

SHOULDERING THE LOAD

Because the shoulder muscles do so much work during a cow's lifetime, they're less marbled than other cuts and feature just a light fat cap. This lean nature makes it an attractive cut for those who want wonderful beef flavour but prefer to avoid the heavier fat content of other beef cuts.

KEEP THE SERVING SIMPLE, OFFERING THE BEEF WITH WHITE BREAD, RED ONIONS, AND PICKLE SLICES.

))) THE SMOKE

1 With the pit temperature stabilized at 120°C (250°F), place the clod into the middle of the pit, pointing the thickest part toward the heat source and with the fat cap facing up.

2 After 14 hours, insert an instant-read thermometer into thickest part of the clod to check the progress. The target temperature for removing clod is 79°C (175°F).

3 When the clod reaches the target temperature, in 4–6 more hours, remove it from the pit. Allow it to rest for up to 1 hour; it will continue to cook and reach the ideal serving temperature of 82°C (180°F).

4 Slice across the grain and portion. (While you can shred it before serving, keep in mind this can cause the meat to dry out much too quickly.)

" **Clod is a big cut, so be sure to have plenty of fuel and wood on hand to keep the smoke going.** "

A RETRO BARBECUE STAPLE
Some old-style American barbecue operations have been cooking clods for generations. These places tend to have started out as meat markets, butchering sides of beef straight from slaughterhouses. If you ever come across an American barbecue restaurant selling clod, have a taste. It's a lean, flavoursome cut that deserves a wider audience.

Meat Beef	**Wood** Oak	**Prep time** 1 hr	**Smoker temp** 120°C (250°F)	**Cook time** 28–40 mins	**Rest time** 10 mins	**Yield** Serves 4

These well-marbled steaks are seared directly on the coals after coming off the pit. So if you're looking to create a show for your guests, invite them to watch you smoke ribeye.

RIBEYE

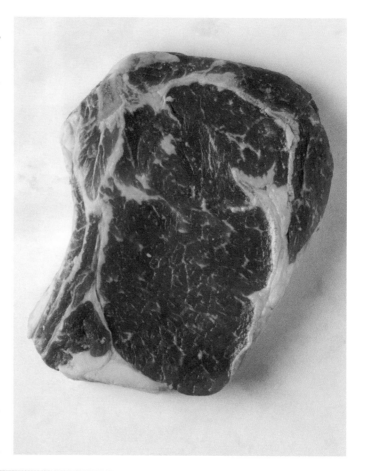

THE MEAT

4 thick-cut ribeye steaks, about 565g (1¼lb) and 5cm (2in) thick each

• Ribeye comes from the forerib section of a cow and has a good marbling of fat.

• This muscle is lightly used, making it tender.

🔥 THE FIRE

Light the pit fire 1 hour before smoking. Add wood 30 minutes before smoking.

• Target temp: 120°C (250°F)

• Wood needs: Low

TEMPERATURE GUIDE			
	Cook time	Pull temp	Serving temp
Rare	28 mins	57°C (135°F)	60°C (140°F)
Medium-rare	30 mins	60°C (140°F)	63°C (145°F)
Medium	35 mins	68°C (155°F)	71°C (160°F)
Medium-well	40 mins	74°C (165°F)	77°C (170°F)

TIME PLAN (2 HRS 18 MINS TO 2 HRS 23 MINS)

30 mins	15 mins	45 mins	28–40 mins	10 mins	10 mins
Build the fire	Make the rub	Rub and rest	Smoke	Rest	Sear

✳ THE RUB

Ingredients

140g (5oz) coarse sea salt
115g (4oz) cracked black pepper

" Ribeyes are sometimes sold with bones in. These steaks –called 'cowboy cut' in America – are more flavoursome, in my opinion, than traditionally cut ribeye steaks off the bone. "

1 Place the steaks on a shallow tray. Season generously with the salt and black pepper and massage the seasonings into both sides.

2 Roll the edges of the steaks in the seasonings in the tray to cover with salt and pepper.

3 Allow the steaks to rest uncovered at room temperature, as below, for 45 minutes before going into the pit.

IT'S BETTER TO RUB RATHER THAN SPRINKLE THE SEASONINGS ON THE MEAT. THAT WAY, YOU ENSURE IT'S THOROUGHLY COATED.

))) THE SMOKE

1 With the pit temperature stabilized at 120°C (250°F), use tongs to place the ribeye steaks into the middle of the pit, leaving ample room between each piece.

2 After 25 minutes, insert an instant-read thermometer into the middle of each steak to check the progress. Remove them from the pit when they reach your ideal target temperature, in 3–10 more minutes.

3 Use a shovel to create a flat spot in the coals. Place the steaks directly on the coals, as above, and sear for 2 minutes per side.

4 Allow the ribeye steaks to rest uncovered for 10 minutes before serving.

ACCOMPANY RIBEYE WITH A GREEN SALAD OR A HEARTIER ASPARAGUS AND TOMATO SALAD.

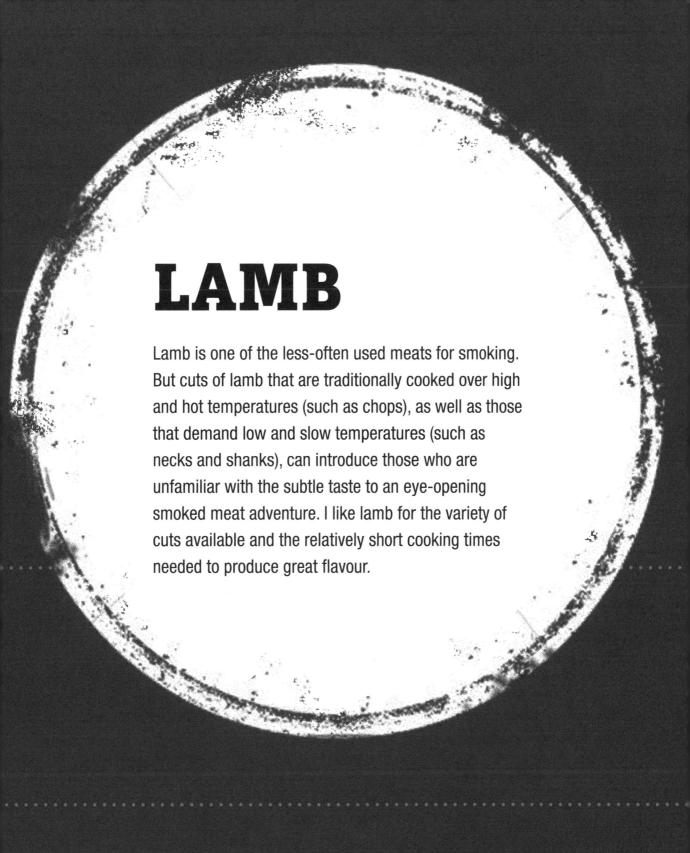

LAMB

Lamb is one of the less-often used meats for smoking. But cuts of lamb that are traditionally cooked over high and hot temperatures (such as chops), as well as those that demand low and slow temperatures (such as necks and shanks), can introduce those who are unfamiliar with the subtle taste to an eye-opening smoked meat adventure. I like lamb for the variety of cuts available and the relatively short cooking times needed to produce great flavour.

SMOKING LAMB: WHAT YOU NEED to KNOW

Lamb cooked on a smoker is a versatile and delicious choice for people who want to venture into new territory. These tips will help you expand what you can do with your smoker and expose you to this underused but exceptionally delicious meat.

IN THE KITCHEN

Successfully smoking lamb starts with buying only high-quality cuts, and learning how to properly season and prepare them for smoking.

Choose top-quality lamb
Look for cuts of lamb that are finely grained with a deep red colour. The fat should appear firm and creamy and any silverskin should be removed. If possible, buy local lamb; it's available year-round and is tastier than frozen meat from far away. Grass-fed lamb offers the best flavour.

Consider an eclectic spice palette
Lamb has a unique flavour that's unlike other meats. Because of this, lamb shouldn't be seasoned in the same way that you might season other meats such as beef or chicken. Subtle herb and spice flavours, such as sage or sumac, are good choices, as are simple salt and pepper. Lamb has a natural sweetness that can also withstand fragrant citrus or hot chillies. Experiment with bold flavours for your rubs with spices such as smoked paprika, cumin, cayenne pepper, or cardamom.

PURCHASE QUALITY CUTS
Things to look for when shopping for lamb

GRADE	SMOKE QUALITY	DESCRIPTION
Organic grass-fed	Excellent	This is the highest quality lamb you can buy. Expect meat that's exceptionally tender, juicy, and very flavoursome, with a high degree of marbling.
Salt marsh	Excellent	Look out for this amazing meat, especially when it comes from Wales or Cornwall. The animals have grazed on seaweed and other sea vegetables, giving the meat incredible seasoning from within.
Free-range lamb	Good	This will probably have less marbling than the cuts above and yield a slightly less juicy or flavoursome cut, but it's still acceptable for smoking.
Supermarket fresh	Poor	This lamb will have even less marbling than the choices above and will likely produce a drier, tougher cut from a smoker.
Supermarket frozen	Poor	This lamb usually has very little marbling, and it generally yields a dry, less flavoursome meat, due to the freezing process.

Experiment with small cuts first

Much as with beef, it's best to start your lamb smoking experiments with smaller cuts first. A good choice for a first-timer smoking lamb is a french-trimmed rack of lamb. While this cut is more expensive than leg shanks, it cooks quickly to 57°C (135°F), and it's easy to gauge its doneness. This is a cut you can serve rare, and is delicious when crusted with fresh herbs.

Strengthen your smoking prowess with larger lamb cuts

Lamb cuts that still have bones – such as leg shanks – are a great place to build on your knowledge about smoking lamb. The foreleg shank is an approachable size, has a decent amount of fat, and cooks evenly because of the hollow bone running through the middle. It needs long, slow cooking because it needs to be tenderized.

ON THE SMOKER

Being armed with some basic knowledge around the smoker will increase your odds for successfully smoking lamb.

Don't overwhelm your lamb cuts with wood flavours

Because lamb has a good natural flavour, you won't want the wood smoke to overpower the rub seasoning mingling with the meat. While a subtle smoke flavour (such as oak or apple) works best, try bold woods (such as hickory or mesquite) on smaller cuts with shorter cooking times for an upfront smoke taste that isn't too overpowering.

Diverse cooking times for lamb still require concentration

Like beef, lamb cuts typically have long smoking times. You could certainly get your smoker to the target temperature and walk away from it for a couple of hours. However, if you're new to smoking lamb, paying attention to how lamb smokes for a smaller cut, such as a rack, will help you better manage the process as you take on bigger cuts.

How to determine when lamb has finished smoking

Recognizing when lamb has finished in the smoker comes with practice, so aim for a day when you can look at lamb or gently touch it with heavy-duty tongs to determine its firmness. Until then, rely on your instant-read thermometer so you learn to know when it is ready.

Always serve lamb hot off the smoker

Unless you're eating it as a late-night snack on pitta bread with tzatziki sauce and roast vegetables, lamb is best served hot off the smoker. Once you've taken it from your smoker, keep it gently wrapped to allow the meat to continue cooking and to stay warm.

Pair with flavoursome sauces and sides

Lamb is a wonderfully rich meat, and it takes to other flavours and foods incredibly well. Pairing lamb with sauces, such as the bourbon plum sauce or sweet-sour black dip featured in this chapter, enhances the flavour of the meat but without overwhelming it. Experiment with different sauces and sides when serving lamb to your guests, but whatever you serve with this meat, it should bring out the best flavours.

Serve lamb cuts with gusto and pride (not fear)

Some people are hesitant to serve lamb, but sometimes a taste of the meat from the smoker is all it takes to convert doubters. If you truly want to expose people to lamb, don't be shy about what you are serving. Letting everyone know what they're about to eat, and showing confidence in how delicious it will be, will do more long-term good, and it will help people truly decide if lamb is something they enjoy.

LAMB CUTS

Lamb is a lean, nutrient-dense, and incredibly delicious meat that is amazingly versatile and flavoursome on the smoker. Understanding which cuts smoke well, and which to avoid on the smoker, will help you make the right purchases as you venture into smoking this under-smoked meat.

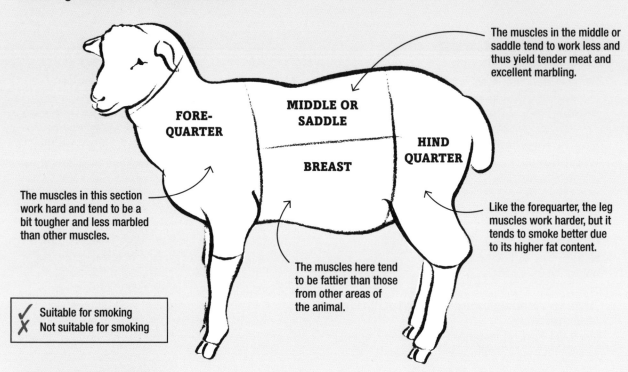

The muscles in the middle or saddle tend to work less and thus yield tender meat and excellent marbling.

FORE-QUARTER

MIDDLE OR SADDLE

HIND QUARTER

BREAST

The muscles in this section work hard and tend to be a bit tougher and less marbled than other muscles.

The muscles here tend to be fattier than those from other areas of the animal.

Like the forequarter, the leg muscles work harder, but it tends to smoke better due to its higher fat content.

✓ Suitable for smoking
✗ Not suitable for smoking

FOREQUARTER

Neck

✓ **Neck:** Containing 3 vertebrae, this rich cut is full of connective tissue that needs to be broken down through low, slow smoking. It is an often-overlooked cut that's very

forgiving to the smoker cook looking to try lamb for the first time. Each lamb neck averages 1.8–2.25kg (4–5lb).

✗ **Front leg:** Also laden with connective tissue and just a small amount of fat, the forelegs are often used for minced lamb and aren't great for smoking.

✓ **Neck fillet:** This runs along the top of the shoulders and is ideal for the low, slow cooking of the smoker, as it contains a good amount of fat.

✓ **Shoulder:** This versatile cut can be rolled and tied and has enough fat to remain succulent throughout longer smoking times. Although shoulder is a bit tougher than other cuts in the forequarter, with proper time it smokes well.

MIDDLE OR SADDLE

Rack

✓ **Rack:** Cut perpendicular to the spine, racks may contain up to 16 ribs; however, most are commonly sold as 8-bone racks. They can be smoked whole and sliced into individual portions, perfect for weekend gatherings.

✓ **Loin:** Cut from along the spine and under the back ribs, this little-used muscle is lean and tender. It benefits from a reverse searing process (see p46) and is cooked to rare temperatures on the smoker.

✓ **Noisette:** While lean, this cut is perhaps the most tender of all lamb cuts and smokes incredibly well. It benefits from a reverse searing technique because of the lack of fat.

✓ **Chop:** This usually includes a rib and a spine section, and they're cut near the spine, resembling centre-cut pork chops. They yield flavoursome meat when smoked.

BREAST

✓ **Breast:** Oblong-shaped with layers of both fat and lean tissue with the fat usually covering one side, the breast is similar to a brisket and can be cooked on a smoker.

✗ **Flank:** From just in front of the rear leg, flank tends to be a tough cut and is most often used for minced lamb. Due to its toughness, flank is not a good choice for smoking.

HINDQUARTER

Shank

✓ **Shank:** The hind shank is located in the middle portion of the leg and is a deliciously fatty, bone-in cut that's a favourite of mine to smoke. The 175–225g (6–8-oz) portion renders very well and has enough fat to remain moist and tender.

✓ **Bone-in or boned and rolled leg:** The rear legs account for around 34 per cent of the total weight of the carcass and are often sold as bone-in cuts. Both boned and rolled leg of lamb and bone-in leg can be an excellent choice for smoking, as they are large and medium-fat cuts that can withstand smoking quite well.

✓ **Steak:** Cut from the sirloin end toward the shank, lamb steaks benefit from reverse searing (see p46) and should be cooked rare to medium rare to remain moist.

LAMB VS. MUTTON
Lamb is, by definition, a sheep slaughtered before reaching 12 months old. The meat is tender when compared to that of older animals, and it has become by far the most commonly eaten sheep meat.

Sheep slaughtered at fewer than 3 months old is sold as "baby" or "milk" lamb. The joints from such an animal will be too small and lean for successful smoking. A "spring" lamb of 4–9 months, or a "winter" lamb of 10–11 months, is of a size that is more suitable for these recipes. Meat from a sheep slaughtered after reaching 1 year old is referred to as *hogget*. Meat from sheep that are older than 2 years are defined as *mutton*.

While both have meat that tends to be tougher than lamb, hogget and mutton nevertheless have a richness of flavour that makes it a preferred smoking meat for some cooks. However, while recent campaigns have tried to revive interest in mutton as a mainstream meat, it's still hard to find outside speciality stores.

Meat Lamb	**Wood** Oak	**Prep time** 1 hr	**Smoker temp** 132°C (270°F)	**Cook time** 45 mins to 1¼ hrs	**Rest time** 25 mins	**Yield** Serves 4

Lamb chops might not be the most obvious item to receive the smoke treatment, but give these a go. They will win your heart… and your stomach.

RACK OF LAMB

THE MEAT

3 racks of lamb, 800g (1¾lb) each

- Racks of lamb are typically sold in 8-bone racks. Depending on the size of the lamb, they will vary slightly in weight.

- Butchers often French-trim the racks, which means removing the fat and tissue between the bones to expose about 5cm (2in) of clean bone.

THE FIRE

Light the pit fire 1 hour before smoking. Add wood 30 minutes before smoking.

- Target temp: 132°C (270°F)

- Wood needs: Low to medium

TEMPERATURE GUIDE

	Cook time	Pull temp	Serving temp
Rare	45 mins	54°C (130°F)	57°C (135°F)
Medium rare	1 hr	60°C (140°F)	63°C (145°F)
Medium	1 hr 15 mins	68°C (155°F)	71°C (160°F)

TIME PLAN (2 HRS 40 MINS TO 3 HRS 10 MINS)

30 mins	15 mins	45 mins	45 mins to 1 hr 15 mins	25 mins
Build the fire	Make the rub	Rub and rest	Smoke	Rest

THE RUB

Ingredients

70g (2¼oz) coarse sea salt
30g (1oz) cracked black pepper
2 tbsp granulated sugar
2 tbsp paprika
1 tbsp ground cumin
1 sprig of fresh rosemary, finely chopped
6 fresh basil leaves, roughly chopped

A LITTLE ABOUT LAMB
Meat from a sheep less than 1 year old is called lamb to distinguish it from that from older sheep (known as hogget or mutton). Because of a lamb's youth and smaller size, connective tissue is less developed, and the meat is therefore more tender and less fatty.

1 In a medium bowl, thoroughly mix the salt, black pepper, sugar, paprika, cumin, fresh rosemary, and fresh basil.

2 Sprinkle an even coating of rub on each lamb rack, and gently pat on all sides with your hands so it sticks. Allow the lamb to rest uncovered at room temperature for 45 minutes before going into the pit.

))) THE SMOKE

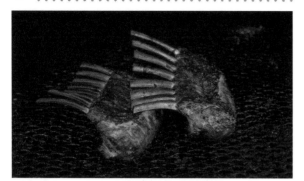

1 With your pit temperature stabilized at 132°C (270°F), use tongs to place the lamb racks in the middle of the pit, bones curved downwards.

2 After 45 minutes, use an instant-read thermometer to check the progress of each lamb rack, being sure to avoid touching the bones with the probe.

3 Remove from the pit when the lamb racks are 2°C (5°F) below your preferred temperature, up to 30 more minutes. Allow the lamb to rest uncovered for 25 minutes before slicing the racks into individual chops.

GAUGING TEMPERATURE
Take the temperature of a lamb rack between the second and third bones rather than in the middle of the rack. Otherwise, your end chops will end up being overcooked.

I LIKE TO PRESENT MY LAMB RACKS IN A BIG SERVING DISH ON THE TABLE, GARNISHED WITH FRESH HERBS.

Meat Lamb	Wood Oak	Prep time 7 days 1 hr	Smoker temp 120°C (250°F)	Cook time 3½ hrs	Rest time 30 mins	Yield Serves 4

My recipe draws inspiration from the old Kentucky barbecue tradition of cooking cuts of mutton – sheep older than 12 months – over low heat on open pits. The sauce here uses bourbon whiskey to add an extra bit of smokiness to the lamb.

LAMB SHANKS with BOURBON PLUM SAUCE

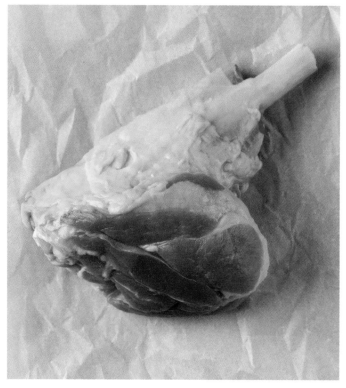

THE MEAT

4 lamb shanks, about 450g (1lb) each

• Lamb shanks are cut from the shoulder or leg bone. Those taken from the leg are larger.

• Always buy fresh lamb, as frozen lamb loses moisture, and therefore flavour.

THE FIRE

Light the pit fire 1 hour before smoking. Add wood 30 minutes before smoking.

• Target temp: 120°C (250°F)

• Wood needs: Medium

TEMPERATURE GUIDE

	Cook time	Pull temp	Serving temp
Well	3 hrs 30 mins	74°C (165°F)	77°C (170°F)

TIME PLAN (7 DAYS 7 HRS)

7 days	30 mins	15 mins	45 mins	3 hrs 30 mins	90 mins	30 mins
Make infusion	Build the fire	Make the rub	Rub and rest	Smoke	Make the sauce	Rest

🖌 THE PREP

Ingredients
2 large plums
240–300ml (8–10fl oz) bourbon whiskey

1 Using a chef's knife, cut the plums into quarters and remove their stones.

2 Place the plums into a scrupulously clean glass jar with a tight-fitting lid, or other non-reactive container. Cover completely with the bourbon.

3 Seal and store the jar in a dark, cool place, gently shaking it once a day for 7 days.

PLANNING AHEAD
The bourbon-plum infusion must sit for 6–7 days before you can use it. Don't open the jar during the infusion process to check it, or to try to speed things along. Allowing air into the jar will prevent the full infusion process from completing, and you'll end up with a flavour you won't enjoy. You simply have to exercise some patience and forward planning to ensure your plum infusion is ready to go before you light the pit fire.

❝ I like to use Jim Beam Kentucky Straight Bourbon Whiskey to make this infusion. This type of bourbon whiskey has been aged for years in charred oak barrels, providing a unique, smoky bite. ❞

HANDLE EACH RUBBED LAMB SHANK BY ITS BONE TO KEEP THE RUB OFF YOUR HANDS.

❊ THE RUB

Ingredients

70g (2¼oz) coarse sea salt
30g (1oz) cracked black pepper
2 tbsp granulated sugar
1 tbsp garlic powder
1 tbsp paprika
1 tbsp ground cumin
2 tsp dried thyme

1 In a medium bowl, combine the salt, black pepper, sugar, garlic powder, paprika, cumin, and dried thyme.

2 Evenly coat the lamb shanks with the rub. Allow them to rest uncovered at room temperature for at least 45 minutes before going into the pit.

THE SAUCE

Ingredients

240–300ml (8–10fl oz) Bourbon-plum Infusion
   (see pp66–67)
1 small red onion, finely chopped
3 tsp Worcestershire sauce
1 tsp freshly ground black pepper
2 sprigs of fresh rosemary, leaves chopped

1 Strain the infused bourbon from its jar into a medium bowl. Remove the whiskey-infused plums from the jar and coarsely chop each piece with a chef's knife.

2 Add the plums to the bowl with the infused bourbon, along with the onion, Worcestershire sauce, black pepper, and rosemary, as above.

3 Pour the mixture into a small saucepan and bring to a simmer over a low heat. Allow to simmer for 1 hour or until the sauce reduces by half. Remove from the heat and allow to cool to room temperature.

))) THE SMOKE

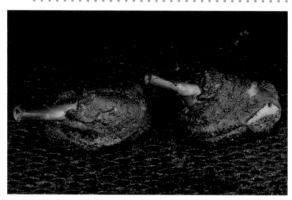

1 With the pit temperature stabilized at 120°C (250°F), use tongs to place the lamb shanks on the middle rack, making sure to point the larger ends toward the heat source, as above.

2 After 2½ hours, use an instant-read thermometer to check each lamb shank's progress, ensuring you don't rest the probe against the bone. The target temperature for removing lamb shanks from the smoker is 74°C (165°F).

3 When the lamb shanks have reached the target temperature, about 1 more hour, remove from the pit. Allow them to rest uncovered for 30 minutes. They will continue to cook and reach the ideal serving temperature of 77°C (170°F), when the meat should pull away easily from the bone.

4 Drizzle the sauce over the lamb shanks with a large spoon and serve.

BETTER WITH THE BONE
Lamb shanks contain a tubular bone that's surrounded by a thin layer of fat. This bone helps in the cooking process because it's filled with marrow that gathers heat more quickly than the surrounding dense protein, allowing the cooking process to begin from the inside.

SERVE THE LAMB SHANKS OVER CREAMY MASHED POTATOES, OR GARNISH WITH FRESH ROSEMARY.

Meat Lamb	Wood Oak	Prep time 1 hr	Smoker temp 120°C (250°F)	Cook time 5½–6 hrs	Rest time 35 mins	Yield Serves 4

The meat of lamb necks has a texture akin to pulled pork. Complementing the lamb here is a tart and tangy dip that cuts through the intense richness.

LAMB NECKS with SWEET–SOUR DIP

 ## THE MEAT

2 lamb necks, about 2kg (4½lb) each

• Lamb necks are cut directly above the animal's shoulder and each piece will contain up to 3 vertebrae.

• Because of the relative toughness of the meat, lamb necks are normally slow-cooked in stews and may be difficult to find in supermarkets; your butcher will be a better source.

THE FIRE

Light the pit fire 1 hour before smoking. Add wood 30 minutes before smoking.

• Target temp: 120°C (250°F)

• Wood needs: Medium to high

TEMPERATURE GUIDE

	Cook time	Pull temp	Serving temp
Well	5½ hrs	74°C (165°F)	77°C (170°F)

TIME PLAN (8 HRS 5 MINS TO 8 HRS 35 MINS)

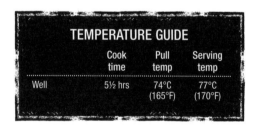

30 mins	15 mins	45 mins	5½–6 hrs	30 mins	35 mins
Build the fire	Make the rub	Rub and rest	Smoke	Make the dip	Rest

 # THE RUB

Ingredients

70g (2¼oz) coarse sea salt
30g (1oz) cracked black pepper
2 tbsp granulated sugar
2 tbsp ground cumin
1 tbsp paprika
1 tbsp garlic powder
1 tsp cayenne pepper

1 In a medium bowl, combine the salt, black pepper, sugar, cumin, paprika, garlic powder, and cayenne pepper.

2 Coat the lamb necks evenly with the rub. Allow them to rest uncovered for at least 45 minutes before going into the pit.

 # THE DIP

Ingredients

120ml (4fl oz) Worcestershire sauce
120ml (4fl oz) cider vinegar
2 tbsp dark brown sugar
1 tbsp lemon juice
½ tsp garlic powder

1 In a small saucepan over a low heat, combine the Worcestershire sauce, cider vinegar, dark brown sugar, lemon juice, and garlic powder.

2 Bring to a simmer, as above, stirring as it heats, until the sugar has dissolved, about 3 minutes. Remove from the heat and set aside until ready to use.

> **While considered by some to be a low-prestige cut, lamb necks have a rich flavour due to the high volume of blood flow through the muscles, the large amounts of connective tissue they contain, and their proximity to the vertebrae.**

))) THE SMOKE

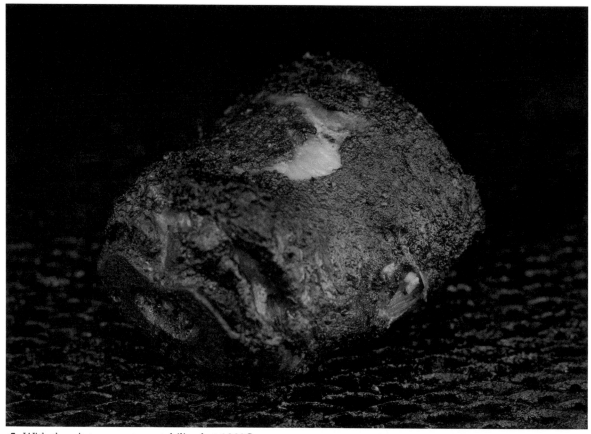

1 With the pit temperature stabilized at 120°C (250°F), use tongs to place the lamb necks on the middle rack, being sure to keep them away from any hot spots.

2 After 4½ hours, insert an instant-read thermometer into the fattest part of each lamb neck to check the progress, making sure the probe doesn't touch the bone. The target temperature for removing lamb necks is 74°C (165°F).

3 When the lamb necks have reached the target temperature, 1–1½ hours more, remove them from the pit. Allow them to rest uncovered for 35 minutes. They will continue to cook and reach the ideal well-done temperature of 77°C (170°F). Serve with the dip (see p73).

SERVE IT YOUR WAY
Serving lamb necks is a great opportunity to put your own twist on this unusual cut. Pulling meat from the bone, dousing it with some of the dip, and stacking it high on a bun – garnished with some sweet pickles – is my favourite way to eat lamb neck.

You can also slice the meat off the bone and serve it like a roast. You may even decide to smother the entire cut in the dip and then eat it with a knife and fork.

IF YOU'RE SERVING PULLED LAMB NECK ON A SANDWICH, BE GENEROUS WITH ACCOMPANIMENTS.

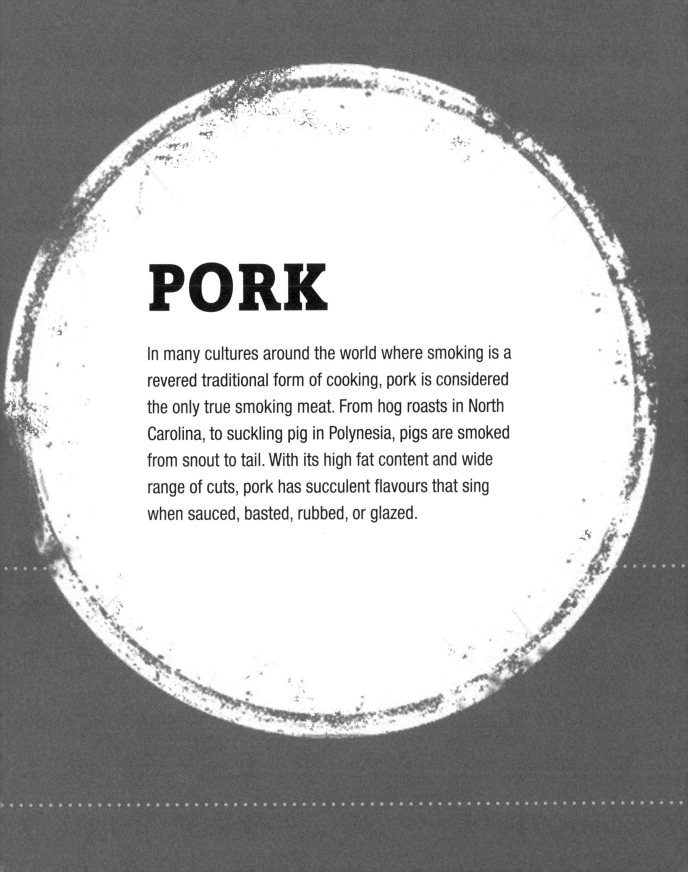

PORK

In many cultures around the world where smoking is a revered traditional form of cooking, pork is considered the only true smoking meat. From hog roasts in North Carolina, to suckling pig in Polynesia, pigs are smoked from snout to tail. With its high fat content and wide range of cuts, pork has succulent flavours that sing when sauced, basted, rubbed, or glazed.

SMOKING PORK: WHAT YOU NEED to KNOW

Pork comprises nearly 40 per cent of the meat consumed globally, and for good reason: it's absolutely delicious. The meat takes to smoke beautifully, and following these tips as you venture into smoking pork will allow you to enjoy it even more.

IN THE KITCHEN

Smoking pork starts with buying only high-quality cuts, and learning how to properly season and prepare them for smoking.

Use colour as a gauge for buying pork

Fresh pork should have an even pink colour and very little fat marbling. Look for a thin line of fat around the sides of chops or roasts and a natural fat cap on fresh (also called *green*) hams.

Season your pork cuts with intent

Pork has such a naturally wonderful taste that mere salt and pepper can suffice. But you can bring out some tantalizing flavours hidden in pork through simple seasonings, such as brown sugar, cumin, or mustard powder, all of which will make your taste buds dance with joy.

Go beyond just barbecue sauce

Slathering pork with barbecue sauce in all its incarnations has become so ingrained in some people's taste experience that offering anything else might seem odd. But don't be afraid to concoct your own creative sauces to help your diners enjoy pork in new ways.

Pork is a safe choice for smoking

Pork has a bad reputation for being too fatty and therefore unhealthy, for harbouring potential bacterial contamination, and for carrying the parasite trichinosis. But pigs today are bred to be nearly 15 per cent leaner, and the conditions they're raised in and the diets they're fed have become more sanitary and modernized.

Watch out for tampering

Avoid pork cuts that have been injected, marinated, or cured by the manufacturer. Hams, hocks or shanks, and pork belly are sold in a variety of packages, and many will mask the fact that the product has been treated with additional additives.

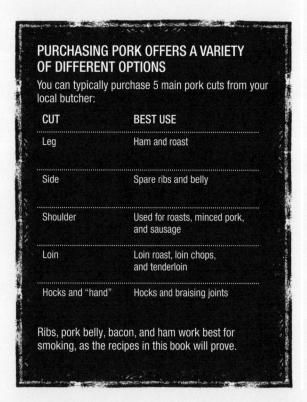

PURCHASING PORK OFFERS A VARIETY OF DIFFERENT OPTIONS

You can typically purchase 5 main pork cuts from your local butcher:

CUT	BEST USE
Leg	Ham and roast
Side	Spare ribs and belly
Shoulder	Used for roasts, minced pork, and sausage
Loin	Loin roast, loin chops, and tenderloin
Hocks and "hand"	Hocks and braising joints

Ribs, pork belly, bacon, and ham work best for smoking, as the recipes in this book will prove.

ON THE SMOKER

A little basic knowledge in the kitchen and around the smoker will increase your odds for successfully smoking pork.

How pigs are raised affects how they smoke

Because pigs don't need much space, they don't have big ecological footprints. However, keeping them in smaller pens also results in their not moving around as much, creating fatter pigs with less flavoursome meat.

Choose wood that best pairs with your pork cut

You can't go wrong when smoking with oak. It burns slowly and hard and offers a solid smoke flavour. But you can also experiment with pecan, hickory, and myriad fruit woods (such as apple or cherry), to enrich your pork cuts.

Smoke pork to minimum temperatures for maximum safety

Myths about pork needing to be well-done have to do with cultural biases and a few well-documented food-borne illness incidents. It is usually recommended to cook pork to 63°C (145°F) to ensure any bacteria or parasites present in the meat are killed. Cooking to this temperature – rather than to the traditional 82°C (180°F) – allows the juices to run clear and the meat to retain a mildly pinkish hue.

Lean pork still requires longer cooking temperatures

As with all pork cuts, the thicker they are, the longer they'll take to smoke. For example, pork shoulder has connective tissue that needs to break down over long, low-temperature cooking. Thus, if an average pork shoulder joint weighs 3.5–4kg (7–8lb), it can take around 5 hours for it to reach 71°C (160°F).

BE CAREFUL TO BUY HIGH-WELFARE PORK, AS INTENSIVELY REARED MEAT IS BOTH CRUEL AND LACKING IN FLAVOUR

Complement your pork, and people will compliment you

You can smoke pork without seasonings or sauces, simply allowing the wood to flavour your meat, and still have a dish worth eating time and time again. But pork can benefit from complementary flavours, such as slicing and serving it with a favourite bread and mustard. That's the beauty you can find through smoking: discovering different things you can do with your smoked cuts.

You should cure and smoke your own bacon

Curing pork belly for home-made bacon is a technique that involves 2 stages: curing in a salt-and-sugar solution to draw moisture from the meat, and then low-temperature cooking. If bacon is refrigerated below 4°C (40°F) during the curing process and then smoked at 82°C (180°F), it's both perfectly safe to eat and absolutely delicious.

PORK CUTS

Pigs are the most widely eaten of all meats, and they yield some of the most delicious and smokeable meat available. The cuts come from 4 primary sections, and each produces its own unique flavours and textures when smoked.

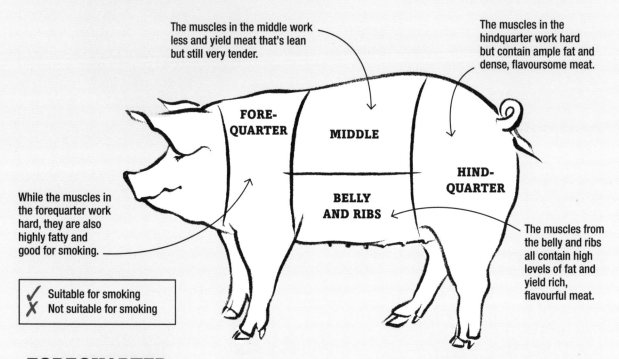

The muscles in the middle work less and yield meat that's lean but still very tender.

The muscles in the hindquarter work hard but contain ample fat and dense, flavoursome meat.

While the muscles in the forequarter work hard, they are also highly fatty and good for smoking.

FORE-QUARTER

MIDDLE

HIND-QUARTER

BELLY AND RIBS

The muscles from the belly and ribs all contain high levels of fat and yield rich, flavourful meat.

✓ Suitable for smoking
✗ Not suitable for smoking

FOREQUARTER

Pork shoulder

✓ **Shoulder:** Containing the shoulder blade, the most common cut of meat from this area of the pig. The shoulder can also be deboned and rolled. This is an excellent choice for smoking because it contains all the fat and connective tissue that breaks down and results in moist, flavoursome smoked meat.

✓ **Hand and spring:** Also known simply as "hand", the hand and spring can be cured and smoked and then served as a substitute for traditional bone-in ham.

✓ **Shank:** The section of the foreleg between the knee and breast, the shank is a fatty and moist cut that's a great choice for smoking.

✗ **Forehock:** Situated below the knee joint, the forehock is lean, typically cured and not particularly well-suited to smoking.

AGE AT SLAUGHTER
Commercially raised pigs are bred to be fast-growing and slaughtered at just 16–17 weeks. Better quality pork is from traditional, slower-growing animals and can be as much as 10 months old. This older meat has had the chance to develop more flavour and a better layer of fat.

MIDDLE

✓ **Loin:** Running below the ribs and along the spine, the loin is a lean cut with a small fat layer, making it ideal for smoking.

✓ **Roast:** Rack of pork, boned and rolled loin, and chump end roasts are all cut from the middle section of the pig. While these cuts are not traditionally thought of as smoking meats, they still smoke well and are ideal for large groups.

Baby back ribs

✓ **Back ribs:** This very common cut of pork consists of 10–13 bones and a decent amount of meat that rests on top of the bones. Ribs are a very good smoking option for first-time smoker cooks, because they cook evenly and in a fairly short amount of time.

✓ **Pork chop:** Cut across the loin, this contains the rib bones from the centre section. Cooked as a larger rack, or individually, this cut is very popular as a smoker item. The fat layer surrounding the chop offers adequate protection from drying out, while the bone promotes even cooking.

BELLY OR RIBS

Spare ribs

✓ **Spare rib:** This cut is taken from the side ribs of the animal towards the front and contains the sternum, cartilage in the tip section, and a little bit of skirt meat. Spare ribs are meaty and flavoursome with a good amount of fat, and take to smoke well.

Belly

✓ **Belly:** Meat from the belly is traditionally cured with a brine solution and is sold as either pork belly or is cold smoked and sold as bacon. Pork belly is a delicious option for smoking, as it contains a balanced amount of lean muscle and fat.

✓ **Belly, thick end meat:** This is the part of the belly from the higher shoulder end, and benefits from its thickness. It is a leaner cut than others from the belly and ribs section, and it has a greater amount of lean meat than fat as compared to the belly. While it isn't the most common cut available, you can smoke it like the belly and produce a great meat. It may not be in your butcher's cabinet, so you may need to order it. It's a less common cut and requires a little more effort to smoke than fattier areas, but it's worth a try.

HINDQUARTER

Leg

✓ **Leg:** The rear leg can be fashioned into an entire ham, and can weigh as much as 11.8–12.7kg (26–28lb). Though it's uncommon to find whole hams this large, smoking a whole leg can be an excellent challenge for the adventurous smoker cook.

✗ **Rump:** This large roasting joint can weigh 1.35–2.25kg (3–5lb). It tends to dry out over longer cooking times and therefore is not appealing for smoking.

✓ **Hind shank:** Taken from the lower portion of the leg above the shank, this will need to be ordered from your butcher. It contains the femur and is a great choice for smoking, as it tends to be less than 5kg (10lb), making it a manageable portion for smaller gatherings.

✓ **Hock:** This meat is popular with smoker cooks because it contains a good amount of fat and connective tissue and cooks evenly both inside and out.

82

Meat Pork	**Wood** Oak or hickory	**Prep time** 1½ hrs	**Smoker temp** 132°C (270°F)	**Cook time** 3½–4 hrs	**Rest time** 20 mins	**Yield** Serves 4

Baby back ribs, very popular both at restaurants and for home barbecues, have a good deal of edible meat and aren't very messy to eat. The fairly uniform shape of each rack promotes even cooking, making this a fairly forgiving cut of pork to smoke.

BABY BACK RIBS

THE MEAT

2 racks of baby back ribs, 1.4kg (3lb) each

• Baby back ribs are cut from just below the spine of a pig and above the spare ribs.

• Typically, butchers cut baby backs into 10–12-bone racks, but you can ask your butcher for a different size, if you prefer.

• Baby back rib bones are 7.5–10cm (3–4in) long, narrowing as each rack tapers toward the pig's back end.

THE FIRE

Light the pit fire 1 hour before smoking. Add wood 30 minutes before smoking.

• Target temp: 132°C (270°F)

• Wood needs: Medium

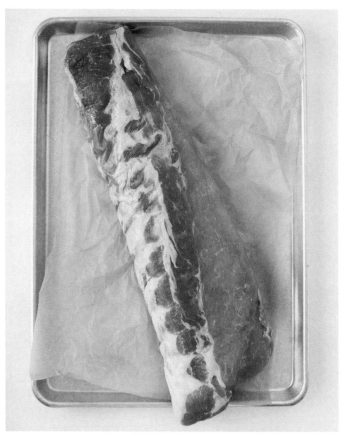

TEMPERATURE GUIDE

	Cook time	Pull temp	Serving temp
Well	3½–4 hrs	77°C (170°F)	77°C (170°F)

TIME PLAN (5 HRS 50 MINS TO 6 HRS 20 MINS)

30 mins	15 mins	45 mins	30 mins	3½–4 hrs		20 mins
Build the fire	Make the rub	Rub and rest	Make the glaze	Smoke		Rest

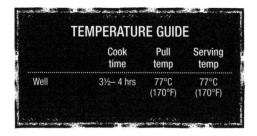

THE PREP

Removing the membrane

On each rib rack, below the curve of the rib bones themselves, is a membrane that can be removed. You have the option of removing the membrane yourself using these steps.

1 Insert a paring knife under an exposed corner of membrane to create a hole large enough for your index finger.

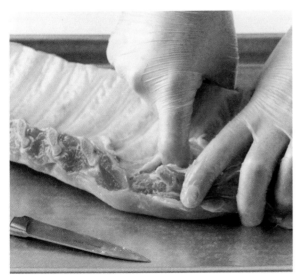

2 Firmly grip the edge of the membrane between your thumb and index finger.

SHOULD YOU REMOVE THE MEMBRANE?
Whether to remove the membrane is the source of hours of debate between barbecue cooks. Some like to leave the membrane intact so rendering fat doesn't run off the racks, thereby maintaining greater moisture. However, others believe that sauce being brushed onto ribs can't penetrate to the meat and impart flavour with the membrane intact, or that the membrane can become tough and leathery. It's a good idea to try cooking baby rack ribs both with and without the membrane to see which method you prefer.

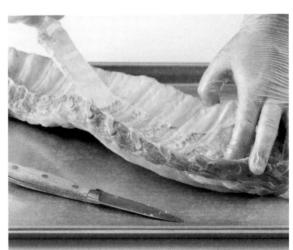

3 Begin peeling away the membrane while holding the rib rack firmly with your opposite hand.

IF YOU BUY THE RIBS FROM A BUTCHER SHOP, YOU CAN ASK THEM TO REMOVE THE MEMBRANE FOR YOU.

THE BROWN SUGAR HELPS CREATE A DEEP, RICH CRUST, WHILE THE CAYENNE PEPPER ADDS A BIT OF BITE.

✳ THE RUB

Ingredients

400g (14oz) dark brown sugar
100g (3½oz) coarse sea salt
1 tbsp cayenne pepper
2 tbsp mustard powder
1 tbsp ground cumin

1 In a medium bowl, combine the dark brown sugar, salt, cayenne pepper, mustard powder, and cumin.

2 Apply the rub to both sides of the rib racks. Allow them to rest uncovered at room temperature for at least 45 minutes before going into the pit.

◗ THE GLAZE

Ingredients

1 litre (1¾ pints) pineapple juice
120ml (4fl oz) cider vinegar
2 tbsp honey
hot pepper sauce, to taste

1 Whisk together the pineapple juice, cider vinegar, honey, and hot pepper sauce to taste.

2 Set the glaze aside until you're ready to baste the rib racks.

> ❝ I prefer to use Tabasco brand hot pepper sauce. However, you can use whatever sauce is your favourite. Also, feel free to increase or decrease the amount of hot sauce you use based on how much heat you want. ❞

))) THE SMOKE

1 With the pit temperature stabilized at 132°C (270°F), use tongs to place the rib racks in the middle of the pit, bone-side down. Be sure to leave at least a finger's width between the racks to allow for good airflow.

2 If using glaze, at the 1½ hour point, add glaze with a brush or mop and then repeat the application 3–4 more times during the remaining cooking time.

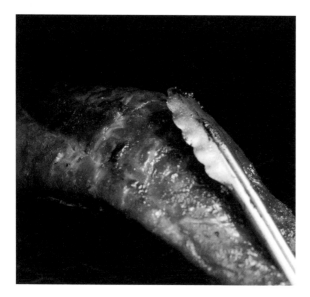

3 After 3½ hours, check the rib racks for doneness by lifting them with tongs, as shown on the left. Rib racks should flex with some separation of bark (crust) and meat, as well as have 5mm (¼in) or less of bone ends exposed.

4 Remove the rib racks from the pit once this flex feels tender and the target temperature has been reached, up to 30 minutes later. Allow them to rest for 20 minutes before cutting into individual bones.

> **I believe ribs shouldn't fall off the bone, but should instead have a toothy tug and not feel mushy when being eaten.**

88

Meat Pork	Wood Oak or pecan	Prep time 1½ hrs	Smoker temp 121°C (250°F)	Cook time 4–5 hrs	Rest time 20 mins	Yield Serves 4

These tender spare ribs, which offer a clean bite and a little bit of a tug when coming away from the bone, are covered in a tangy glaze for truly mouth-watering flavour.

SPARE RIBS

THE MEAT

2 racks of spare ribs, 1.6kg (3½lb) each

• Spare rib racks are large, flat ribs from the pig's sides that are cut away from baby back ribs. Unlike baby back ribs, much of the meat is found between the bones, rather than on top.

• An added bonus is that spare ribs contain the tasty rib tips, which are located just past the end of the lower portion of the rib bones.

• Keep in mind that more than half the weight of spare ribs will be bone.

THE FIRE

Light the pit fire 1 hour before smoking. Add wood 30 minutes before smoking.

• Target temp: 121°C (250°F)

• Wood needs: Medium

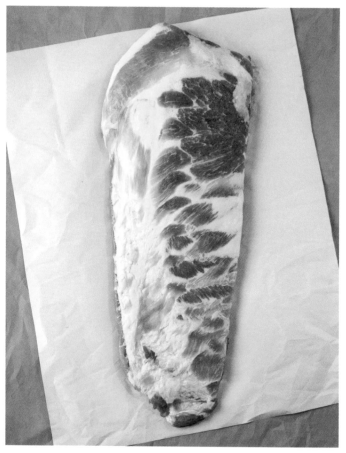

TEMPERATURE GUIDE

	Cook time	Pull temp	Serving temp
Well	4–5 hrs	77°C (170°F)	82°C (180°F)

TIME PLAN (6 HRS 20 MINS TO 6 HRS 50 MINS)

30 mins	15 mins	45 mins	30 mins	4–5 hrs	20 mins
Build the fire	Make the rub	Rub and rest	Make the glaze	Smoke	Rest

✺ THE RUB

Ingredients

400g (14oz) dark brown sugar
200g (7oz) granulated sugar
70g (2¼oz) coarse sea salt
60g (2oz) cracked black pepper or coarsely
  ground black pepper
1 tbsp cayenne pepper
1 tbsp garlic powder
1 tbsp onion powder
2 tsp celery salt

REMOVING THE MEMBRANE
As with baby back ribs, you can choose to
peel the membrane from the underside of
spare rib racks (see p83). This may be your
preference if you plan to brush them with the
glaze overleaf, or a barbecue sauce.

1 In a medium bowl, combine the dark brown
sugar, granulated sugar, salt, black pepper,
cayenne pepper, garlic powder, onion powder,
and celery salt.

2 Apply the rub to both sides of the rib racks. Allow them to rest uncovered
at room temperature for 45 minutes before going into the pit.

THE GLAZE

Ingredients

240ml (8fl oz) tomato ketchup
2 tbsp cider or apple juice
2 tbsp Worcestershire sauce
1 tsp mustard powder
1 tsp ground cumin
1 tsp onion powder
1 tsp garlic powder

1 In a medium bowl, whisk together the tomato ketchup, cider, Worcestershire sauce, mustard powder, cumin, onion powder, and garlic powder until smooth.

2 Set aside until you're ready to glaze the ribs.

THE SMOKE

1 With your pit temperature stabilized at 121°C (250°F), use tongs to place the rib racks in the middle of the pit. Be sure to leave at least a finger's width between the racks to allow for airflow.

2 After 2 hours, working quickly with a mop or brush, apply a thin but even layer of glaze to both sides of each rib rack, as above. Apply the glaze at 30-minute intervals from now on.

3 After 2 more hours, check rib racks for doneness by lifting them with tongs. Rib racks should flex with some separation of bark (crust) and meat, and have 5mm (¼in) or less of bone ends exposed.

4 Remove the racks from the pit once this flex feels tender, 30 minutes to 1 hour later. Allow them to rest uncovered for 20 minutes before cutting them into individual bones.

TESTING DONENESS

Because of the size of the bones and how much meat is sandwiched between them, tenderness is best tested by lifting each rack with your tongs and checking the flex. Lift the rib racks in the middle and pay attention to any splits in the top surface. The rib racks should feel flexible but not springy when lifted.

SPARE RIBS ARE DELICIOUS DRY (WITHOUT SAUCE) OR DIPPED INTO A SWEET AND TANGY BARBECUE SAUCE.

92

Meat Pork	**Wood** Oak or pecan	**Prep time** 1½ hrs	**Smoker temp** 135°C (275°F)	**Cook time** 5½–6 hrs	**Rest time** None	**Yield** Serves 10–12

In this recipe, smoke is woven through the moist meat, while the addition of a mustard and vinegar glaze gives the pulled pork a delicious bite.

PULLED PORK SHOULDER

 ## THE MEAT

1 pork shoulder (neck end), about 2.7kg (6lb)

• Pork shoulder is most commonly used for pulled pork because it has a good deal of connective tissue and fat.

• Pork shoulder extends from the neck, below the spine, down to just above the hand and spring. It contains the shoulder blade that's typically exposed on the end of the cut.

• Depending on the size of the pig, this cut can weigh 2.25–5kg (5–10lb).

THE FIRE

Light the pit fire 1 hour before smoking. Add wood 30 minutes before smoking.

• Target temp: 135°C (275°F)

• Wood needs: Medium to high

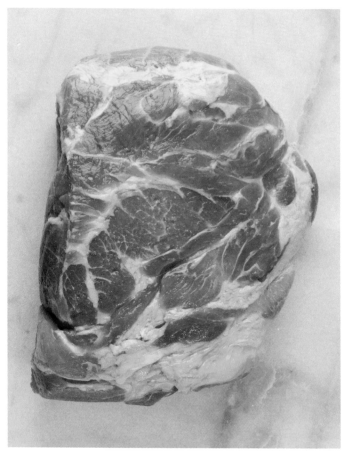

TEMPERATURE GUIDE

	Cook time	Pull temp	Serving temp
Well	5½ hrs	91°C (195°F)	91°C (195°F)

TIME PLAN (7 HRS 45 MINS TO 8 HRS 15 MINS)

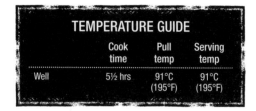

30 mins	15 mins	45 mins	30 mins	5½–6 hrs	15 mins
Build the fire	Make the rub	Rub and rest	Make the glaze	Smoke	Pull pork

✸ THE RUB

Ingredients

400g (14oz) dark brown sugar
70g (2¼oz) coarse sea salt
5 tsp mustard powder
3 tsp smoked paprika
1½ tsp onion powder
1½ tsp garlic powder
1 tsp cayenne pepper

LOOK FOR BONE-IN PORK SHOULDER
Some butchers may remove the shoulder blade. However, I suggest buying pork shoulder with the blade left in, as being able to easily slide the bone out of the shoulder is a good gauge of doneness.

1 In a medium bowl, combine the dark brown sugar, salt, mustard powder (I prefer Colman's mustard powder), smoked paprika, onion powder, garlic powder, and cayenne pepper.

2 Apply the rub to all sides of the pork shoulder, patting it into the surface with your fingers. Allow it to rest uncovered at room temperature for 45 minutes before going into the pit.

THE PORK CAN BE RESTED IN THE REFRIGERATOR OVERNIGHT. JUST BE SURE TO RETURN IT TO ROOM TEMPERATURE BEFORE SMOKING.

● THE GLAZE

Ingredients

750ml (1¼ pints) cider vinegar
180g (6oz) Dijon mustard
1 tbsp granulated sugar
1 tbsp coarse sea salt
3 tsp freshly ground black pepper

1 In a medium bowl, whisk together the cider vinegar, Dijon mustard, sugar, salt, and black pepper until well mixed.

2 Set aside until ready to glaze the pork.

❝ As far as I'm concerned, one of the best parts of pulled pork is the crisp, smoky bark formed on the meat's outside. While most traditional pulled pork is glazed throughout the last several hours of smoking to add an additional layer of flavour, I prefer not to glaze the meat during the cooking process because of how it softens the bark layer. ❞

〰 THE SMOKE

1 With your pit temperature stabilized at 135°C (275°F), use tongs to place the pork shoulder, fat-side up, in the middle of the pit.

2 After 3 hours, working quickly with a mop or brush, apply a thin but even layer of glaze to the pork, and then insert an instant-read thermometer to check the progress. The target temperature for removing pork shoulder is 91°C (195°F).

3 When the pork shoulder has reached the target temperature, 2½–3 hours more, remove from the pit. (The outer layer should be a rich dark brown.)

NO RESTING NECESSARY
With pulled pork, you don't need to worry about it continuing to cook while it rests as you do with other smoked meats. You can pull the pork when its internal temperature reaches 91°C (195°F) without resting it.

GLAZING THE PORK SHOULDER HELPS KEEP THE CRUST MOIST.

4 Working with large forks or meat claws, pull apart the pork shoulder while it's still hot off the pit. Pour the remaining glaze over the meat and serve immediately.

YOU CAN SERVE
PULLED PORK LOOSE
OR ON TOASTED BUNS.
I LIKE IT WITH THINLY
SLICED PICKLES AND
HOT PEPPER SAUCE.

Meat
Pork

Wood
Oak

Prep time
1 hr

Smoker temp
150°C
(300°F)

Cook time
1½ hrs

Rest time
10 mins

Yield
Serves 4

Smoking pork belly produces moist, tender, silky bites that are rich from its plentiful rendered fat. The seasonings in the rub add a bright pop of flavour.

PORK BELLY

THE MEAT

Boneless pork belly, skin on, about 450g (1lb)

• Pork belly is composed of skin, fat, and thin layers of meat from the sides of the pig.

• Slabs of pork belly can be as large as 3.5kg (7lb); however, 450g (1lb) pieces are much more practical for slicing and serving.

• If you buy your pork belly from a butcher, ask them to measure and cut a 450g (1lb) piece with the skin intact.

• Pork belly, when cured, becomes bacon.

THE FIRE

Light the pit fire 1 hour before smoking. Add wood 30 minutes before smoking.

• Target temp: 150°C (300°F)

• Wood needs: Low to medium

TEMPERATURE GUIDE			
	Cook time	Pull temp	Serving temp
Well	1½ hrs	71°C (160°F)	77°C (170°F)

TIME PLAN (3 HRS 25 MINS)

30 mins	15 mins	45 mins	1½ hrs	15 mins	10 mins
Build the fire	Make the rub	Rub and rest	Smoke	Sear	Rest

❋ THE RUB

Ingredients

400g (14oz) dark brown sugar
200g (7oz) granulated sugar
70g (2¼oz) coarse sea salt
60g (2oz) cracked black pepper or coarsely
   ground black pepper
1 tbsp smoked paprika
1 tbsp garlic powder
1 tbsp onion powder

THE OVERNIGHT CURE
If time permits, rub the pork belly and let it rest uncovered in the refrigerator overnight. This extra rest time will intensify the flavour notes of the rub. Be sure to allow it to come back to room temperature before smoking.

1 In a large bowl, mix the dark brown sugar, granulated sugar, salt, black pepper, smoked paprika, garlic powder, and onion powder.

2 Apply the rub liberally to all sides of the pork belly.

3 Allow the pork belly to rest uncovered at room temperature for at least 45 minutes before going into the pit.

))) THE SMOKE

1 With the pit temperature stabilized at 150°C (300°F), use tongs to place the pork belly in a hot spot on your pit that's closer to the heat source, see right.

2 After 45 minutes, insert an instant-read thermometer into the pork belly to check the progress. The target temperature for removing pork belly is 71°C (160°F).

3 When the pork has reached the target, after about 30 more minutes, remove it from the pit.

" I cook pork belly hotter than other proteins because I like the crisp texture that comes from the small pieces of the exposed, rendering fat. **"**

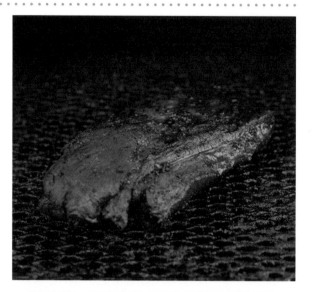

4 Heat a cast-iron pan on the top of your barbecue (you can also do this on the hob in a frying pan). Place the pork belly, skin-side down, into the pan, and cook for about 1 minute. Remove and allow to rest uncovered for 10 minutes before slicing.

SLICE PORK
BELLY THINLY AND
SERVE AS IS OR
IN TOASTED BUNS.

Meat Pork	**Wood** Hickory	**Prep time** 7 days, 30 mins	**Smoker temp** 107°C (225°F)	**Cook time** 2 hrs	**Rest time** 30 mins	**Yield** 25 slices

Curing and smoking your own bacon is a simple and fun process, and once you've tasted the real thing, you'll never go back to eating the commercially processed stuff again.

HOW to CURE and SMOKE BACON

Hot smoking is the key

Making amazing bacon in your smoker is simple, and it's well worth the effort. My recipe uses basic ingredients and doesn't use Prague Powder, an additive used in commercially produced bacon that gives it a fake pink colour and a minerally taste. My recipe uses sea salt and other basic ingredients that allow the meat's natural colour and fat and the smoke to blend, creating a beautiful caramel-brown appearance to the bacon.

This bacon is hot smoked rather than cold smoked, as is traditional. That's because cold-smoked bacon is usually smoked at 38°C (100°F) for 1 hour and then the temperature is reduced to 27°C (80°F) or 32°C (90°F) for 5–6 hours. Such low temperatures bring myriad risks relating to the safety and storage of the finished product. Bacterial growth is nothing to take lightly, making hot smoking the safer process.

> ### APPEARANCE OF CURING PORK BELLY
> Don't be alarmed as the colour of the bacon changes in the refrigerator. After the first few hours, liquid will develop in the bag and some of the salt and sugar will dissolve. As the days progress, you'll notice the colour of the lean part of the pork belly – the meat – begin to turn darker in hue. This is a natural result of the curing process.

PREP

Ingredients
500g (1lb 2oz) coarse sea salt
200g (7oz) light brown sugar
60g (2oz) cracked black pepper
450g (1lb) uncured pork belly
1 tbsp coarsely ground black pepper (optional)

1 In a 3.75 litre (6½ pint) zip-lock plastic bag, mix the salt, light brown sugar, and cracked black pepper.

2 If your pork belly has its skin intact, starting at a corner, insert a sharp, thin knife.

3 Begin to peel the skin back. Allow your knife to follow the uppermost fat layer just beneath the skin, so it comes off easily.

4 Place the pork belly in the bag and squeeze gently, turning it to evenly coat the piece. Gently squeeze out the air from the bag and tightly seal it.

5 Place the bag on a small tray in your refrigerator. Turn the bag over once per day for 7 days. After 7 days, remove the pork belly from the bag and lightly rinse away the flavourings. If desired, dust the cured pork belly with the coarsely ground black pepper. Allow the pork belly to come to room temperature before placing it into the smoker.

〰 SMOKE

1 Once your pit temperature has stabilized at 107°C (225°F), use tongs to place the cured pork belly in the middle of the smoker rack, away from any potential hot spots.

2 After 1½ hours, insert an instant-read thermometer into the pork belly to check the process. Remove from the pit when it reaches 63°C (145°F), about 30 more minutes.

3 Rest the bacon for 30 minutes or until cool to the touch; it will continue to cook to the target temperature of 66°C (150°F).

4 To serve, slice to your preferred thickness, then fry or bake it as desired.

> ❝ Who doesn't love a good piece of bacon? It is easy to make and is something that anyone with a smoker can be proud of serving. ❞

SERVING AND STORING BACON
Unlike cold-smoked bacon that has to be cooked before eating, hot-smoked bacon is ready to eat right from your smoker; however, I recommend cooling, slicing, then cooking it like traditional bacon in a hot cast-iron frying pan. You could also bake it in a preheated oven at 180°C (350°F) for 10–15 minutes. Your cured bacon will last for up to 2 weeks in the refrigerator; wrap it tightly in cling film and then in foil.

Meat Pork	**Wood** Hickory	**Prep time** 1 hr	**Smoker temp** 150°C (300°F)	**Cook time** 3–4 hrs	**Rest time** 40 mins	**Yield** Serves 8–10

More and more, ham is becoming a regular main dish rather than a holiday-only treat. Smoked ham is great straight out of the smoker, or even better as leftovers.

HAM

THE MEAT

Uncured, bone-in half ham, about 3.5kg (7lb)

• Ham comes from a pig's hind leg. Meat from the fore leg is called hand and spring.

• You can smoke both cooked and uncooked hams, though an uncooked ham is ideal for this.

• Some hams can be overly salty and need soaking for 4–6 hours. Your butcher will be able to tell you how much soaking is necessary, though many modern hams don't need any.

🔥 THE FIRE

Light the pit fire 1 hour before smoking. Add wood 30 minutes before smoking.

• Target temp: 150°C (300°F)

• Wood needs: Medium to high

TEMPERATURE GUIDE			
	Cook time	Pull temp	Serving temp
Well	3 hrs	66°C (150°F)	71°C (160°F)

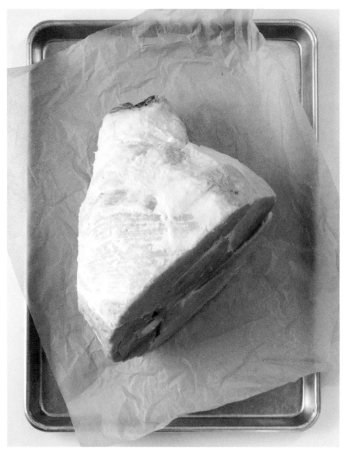

TIME PLAN (4 HRS 25 MINS TO 5 HRS 25 MINS)

30 mins	15 mins	45 mins	3–4 hrs	40 mins	15 mins
Build the fire	Make the rub	Rub and rest	Smoke	Rest	Slice

🌸 THE RUB

Ingredients

600g (1¼lb) dark brown sugar
30g (1oz) coarse sea salt
25g (scant 1oz) mustard powder
2 tbsp garlic powder
2 tbsp onion powder
1 tsp smoked paprika

2 In a medium bowl, mix the dark brown sugar, salt, dry mustard powder, garlic powder, onion powder, and smoked paprika.

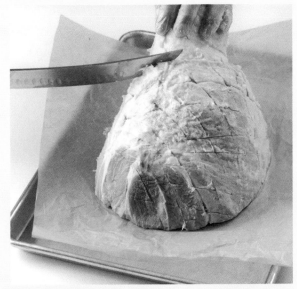

1 Using a sharp knife, score the ham in a criss-cross diagonal pattern, making only light incisions on the surface. Set aside.

WHY SCORE THE HAM?

Scoring the surface of the ham creates a better surface for the rub to adhere to, as well as making for a more attractive presentation when the ham comes off the pit.

3 Liberally apply the rub to the entire surface of the ham, being sure to work it into each incision. Allow to rest uncovered at room temperature for at least 45 minutes before going into the pit.

))) THE SMOKE

1 With the pit temperature stabilized at 150°C (300°F), place the ham in the middle of the rack, ensuring the largest end is positioned closest to the heat source.

2 After 2 hours, insert an instant-read thermometer into the ham to check the progress, making sure the probe doesn't touch the bone. The target temperature for removing the ham is 66°C (150°F).

3 When it has reached the target temperature, about 1 more hour, remove from the pit. Allow to rest uncovered for at least 40 minutes; it will continue to cook and reach the ideal serving temperature of 71°C (160°F).

4 Slice the ham from the bone by making cuts around the outside of the bone.

THIS SWEET AND SMOKY HAM IS DELICIOUS WHEN SLICED THIN FOR SANDWICHES, HOT OR COLD.

POULTRY

Poultry offers smoker cooks an amazing blank canvas. This affordable meat can be brined, injected, sauced, stuffed, or skewered, allowing it to take on an almost unlimited range of flavours from the smoking and seasoning processes. And with recipes that require only short to medium cooking times, smoking poultry provides you with the ideal opportunity to learn more about your smoker and temperature control.

SMOKING POULTRY: WHAT YOU NEED to KNOW

Poultry can provide you with an exciting smoking experience because it tends to cook quickly and can be infused with flavour in many ways. Follow these tips and tricks while experimenting and you'll be smoking delicious birds in no time.

IN THE KITCHEN

Successfully smoking poultry starts with purchasing high-quality birds and adjusting the seasonings based on the type of bird you want to smoke.

Always choose fresh poultry over frozen

When buying poultry, choosing fresh birds or pieces – such as breasts, thighs, or wings – is always better than choosing frozen. Fresh poultry retains more moisture during cooking, whereas previously frozen birds tend to release valuable moisture during the thawing process.

Avoid using boneless and skinless poultry cuts for smoking

Boneless and skinless poultry cuts aren't usually a good choice for low and slow cooking in a smoker because they dry out quickly. Most of these lean cuts will become a dry, leathery abomination that no amount of brining, seasoning, or saucing can save.

Choose wild game wisely

Wild birds are more strongly flavoured poultry choices than farm-raised birds. Their high activity levels make them exceptionally lean, with very little fat content and stouter connective tissues, that can cause them to become tough and prone to drying out on the smoker.

Shop around when sourcing game

Higher-end grocery stores stock game birds that are farm raised, but they're typically pre-frozen because the demand for them is much lower than for other more common poultry items. If you want

PURCHASE QUALITY CUTS
Avoid poor-quality poultry.

GRADE	SMOKE QUALITY	DESCRIPTION
Organic or free-range	Excellent	This is probably the only poultry you'll want to smoke. It has to meet high standards for welfare, resulting in powerful and large legs and juicy, gamey meat.
Anything else, including 'corn-fed', 'farm-raised', and so on	Poor	Sadly, still the most common poultry sold in supermarkets. There is no way to easily tell what welfare standards have been applied, and the meat will be insipid and flabby.

fresh, depending on your location, you may find local shoots that can source the birds for you. There are also many reputable online sellers that sell fresh game birds.

Don't wash your poultry before smoking
Recommendations suggest you shouldn't rinse poultry, because it can actually spread more bacteria than cleaning destroys. Some experts suggest that a better way to help kill bacteria is to treat the poultry with a gentle but effective brine solution, or lightly brush the meat with vinegar to help kill off bacteria without adding flavour.

Brine poultry with caution
Brining poultry can add moisture and deeply seasoned flavour to poultry cuts. However, brines have their limits and should be used prudently.

Overly salted water can turn the bird into an overseasoned disaster that tastes of ham. Start with the goal of imparting mild seasoning and pay careful attention to how long and how heavily you brine your poultry, so you don't end up with something that's inedible.

Sauces and rubs will keep poultry moist
Another effective way to keep poultry from drying out while smoking is to baste the meat with a sauce, that can add a protective moisture barrier. Marinades or rubs can also create barriers that prevent the meat from taking on too much heat and losing excess moisture during the process.

ON THE SMOKER

Following these simple guidelines while smoking poultry will help ensure that your birds come out smoky and juicy.

Select flavoursome wood
Because poultry is generally mild flavoured, smoke can overwhelm its natural flavours. Use a mild wood, such as apple, if you want to complement the natural flavours of chicken or turkey breast. However, if you enjoy bold smoke flavours and are less concerned with the natural flavours of the meat, mesquite-smoked chicken can really pack a flavourful punch.

Avoid temperature spikes and use a water pan
Because poultry is a lean meat, you need to keep the temperature stable throughout the cooking time. If your temperature swings 5°C (10°F) or more when adding fuel, you can dry out the meat if the fat that protects the protein has melted from too much heat. Adding a water pan to the smoker will also help with moisture.

Watch cooking times closely
With the exception of large turkeys (5kg / 10lb and upwards), cooking times are short for whole birds compared with other meats of similar size and weight. For instance, a whole bird needs to reach 66°C (150°F) in the breast to remain juicy. This will occur fairly quickly because the muscle fibres in poultry are stretched and not as densely structured, so they tend to cook faster.

Crisping the skin adds a unique texture
If you prefer, you can put uncooked poultry on a hot grill to crisp the skin before smoking, or you can put smoked poultry on the grill to create that crisp texture.

Spatchcocking will shorten cook times
Spatchcocking birds will help shorten cooking times and ensure even cooking by exposing more of a bird's surface to the heat, whether you're smoking or searing. If you choose to do this, you'll want to really watch the bird to ensure it doesn't cook too quickly and thus dry out.

POULTRY CUTS

All birds, including chicken, turkey, duck, and wild game birds such as pheasant are generally broken into 3 main sections: breast, wing, and leg. The smoking quality of each bird can vary based on the individual traits of the bird, how it was raised, and if it's wild or domestic, but the cuts and their properties are generally the same for all types.

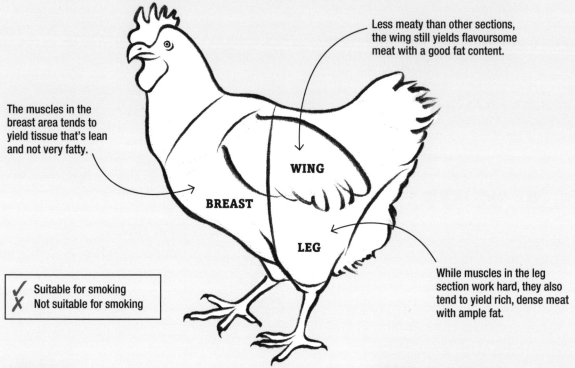

Less meaty than other sections, the wing still yields flavoursome meat with a good fat content.

The muscles in the breast area tends to yield tissue that's lean and not very fatty.

WING

BREAST

LEG

While muscles in the leg section work hard, they also tend to yield rich, dense meat with ample fat.

✓ Suitable for smoking
✗ Not suitable for smoking

WHOLE

Whole chicken

✓ **Whole bird:** Although certain cuts of a bird may not work well when smoked on their own, a whole, intact bird often works incredibly well on a smoker because fattier parts tend to insulate less fatty parts, and the skin tends to keep the whole bird moist.

INTENSIVE VS. FREE-RANGE FARMING

Intensive farming uses machinery and fertilizers to return maximum yields, while free-range farming allows livestock to be kept in natural conditions with freedom of movement. While free-range poultry is more expensive, it tends to have better flavour and texture than intensively farmed birds and is the better choice.

BREAST

Boneless, skinless breast

✗ **Boneless, skinless breast:** As a general rule, this is a poor choice for smoking because it has very little fat and the removed skin will allow the cut to dry out very quickly on a smoker. Turkey breast tends to be larger and more smokeable, and because of their higher fat content, duck breasts are also suitable for smoking.

✗ **Breast fillet:** This refers to a breast with the wing removed. A very lean cut, it is not a great choice for smoking due to its lack of fat.

✗ **Breast quarter:** Containing the breast quarter, wing, and back, and often sold as a barbecue meat, this cut is very lean and isn't a good option for smoking low and slow.

WING

Whole wing

Drummette

✓ **Whole wing:** This all-white meat portion is composed of 3 sections: drumette, middle wing, and tip. These cuts can be smoked as a whole and will even develop a nice crisp skin.

✓ **Drumette:** This first section between the shoulder and the elbow is typically smoked for chicken wings. Drumettes from smaller birds, such as pheasant or quail, aren't suitable for smoking.

✓ **Middle wing:** This refers to the section between the elbow and tip. The two bones found in this cut are often used along with chicken drumettes as chicken wing preparations. While the middle wing is not heavy with meat, the ample fat content and rich, tender meat takes to smoke well, and the skin keeps the meat moist and tender through the smoking process.

LEG

Whole leg

Thigh

Drumstick

✓ **Whole leg:** The whole leg is the drumstick-thigh combination, and it differs from the leg quarter in that it doesn't contain a portion of the back. Chicken leg quarters and duck leg quarters are great options for smoking.

✓ **Thigh:** The thigh is the portion of the leg above the knee joint, and is ideal for smoking due to its high fat content and layering of skin, which helps keep the thigh from drying out during cooking.

✓ **Drumstick:** This cut includes the lower portion of the leg quarter between the knee joint and the hock. Drumsticks of all types are meaty and produce juicy, tender results on the smoker.

Meat Poultry	Wood Oak	Prep time 1 hr	Smoker temp 121°C (250°F)	Cook time 4–4½ hrs	Rest time 30 mins	Yield Serves 6–7

Turkey has developed a bad reputation for being dry and flavourless, but this is only the fault of bad cooking. When smoked, it has amazing flavour and is wonderfully versatile.

TURKEY BREAST

THE MEAT

2 large turkey breasts, skinned, 1.35–1.5kg (3–3¼lb) each

• I recommend buying fresh turkey breast from a butcher. Commercially packaged turkey from a supermarket is typically injected with water that contains salt and preservatives (and for which you will pay by weight).

• Turkey breast tends to be a forgiving meat. The more experience you have with this cut, the easier it becomes to gauge doneness.

THE FIRE

Light the pit fire 1 hour before smoking. Add wood 30 minutes before smoking.

• Target temp: 121°C (250°F)

• Wood needs: Medium

TEMPERATURE GUIDE

	Cook time	Pull temp	Serving temp
Well	4 hrs	74°C (165°F)	82°C (180°F)

TIME PLAN (6¼–6¾ HRS)

30 mins	15 mins	45 mins	4–4½ hrs	30 mins	15 mins
Build the fire	Make the rub	Rub and rest	Smoke	Rest	Slice

❋ THE RUB

Ingredients

50g (1¾oz) light brown sugar
2 tbsp paprika
2 tsp coarsely ground black pepper
2 tsp coarse sea salt
1 tsp garlic powder
1 tsp onion powder
½ tsp cayenne pepper
½ tsp dried sage
½ tsp dried thyme

FOR A MORE INTENSE FLAVOUR, LEAVE RUBBED TURKEY BREASTS IN THE REFRIGERATOR OVERNIGHT.

1 In a medium bowl, combine the light brown sugar, paprika, black pepper, salt, garlic powder, onion powder, cayenne pepper, dried sage, and dried thyme, until well mixed.

2 Apply the rub evenly over all sides of the turkey breasts.

3 Allow the turkey breasts to rest uncovered at room temperature, as below, for at least 45 minutes before going into the pit.

))) THE SMOKE

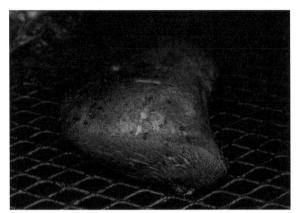

1 With your pit temperature stabilized at 121°C (250°F), use tongs to place the turkey breasts in the centre of the pit and away from any hot spots, with the larger ends pointing towards the heat source.

2 After 3 hours, insert an instant-read thermometer in the centre of the breasts to check the progress. The target temperature for removing turkey breasts is 74°C (165°F).

3 When the turkey breasts have reached the target temperature, after 1–1½ hours more, remove from the pit. Allow to rest, as above, for at least 30 minutes; they will continue to cook and reach the ideal serving temperature of 82°C (180°F).

4 Carve the turkey breasts, on a slight angle, from the larger end toward the smaller end.

SERVE TURKEY BREAST WITH YOUR FAVOURITE BREAD AND CONDIMENT, COMPLEMENTING IT WITH A SAVOURY SIDE DISH OR GARNISHING IT WITH SLICED RED ONION AND JALAPEÑOS.

Meat Poultry	**Wood** Pecan	**Prep time** 1¼ hrs	**Smoker temp** 121°C (250°F)	**Cook time** 45 mins	**Rest time** 10 mins	**Yield** Serves 4

Quail is an interesting bird to smoke because the flesh can take on myriad flavours from different rubs or stuffings, and the meat is consistently tender and moist. It's also very convenient to smoke, due to the relatively short cooking time.

CHILLI QUAIL

THE MEAT

8 spatchcocked quail, 225g (½lb) each

• An average quail yields about 140g (5oz) of meat when cooked whole. Thus a hungry adult might want to enjoy 2 whole birds; bear this in mind when preparing them.

• Spatchcocking is the process of removing the sternum and backbone of a bird and flattening it before cooking.

THE FIRE

Light the pit fire 1 hour before smoking. Add wood 30 minutes before smoking.

• Target temp: 121°C (250°F)

• Wood needs: Low

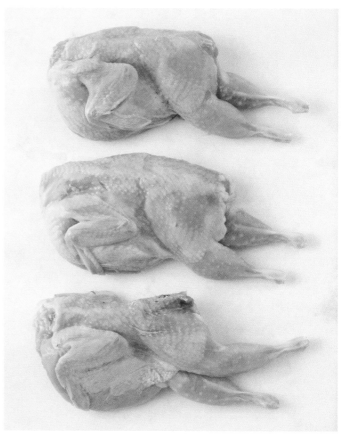

TEMPERATURE GUIDE

	Cook time	Pull temp	Serving temp
Well	45 mins	71°C (160°F)	74°C (165°F)

TIME PLAN (2 HRS 40 MINS)

30 mins	15 mins	15 mins	45 mins	45 mins	10 mins
Build the fire	Make the rub	Prep the quail	Rub and rest	Smoke	Rest

❀ THE RUB

Ingredients

140g (5oz) coarse sea salt
30g (1oz) cracked black pepper
1 tsp dried sage
1 tsp cayenne pepper
8 medium jalapeño peppers
2 crisp, tart apples (such as Fuji or Pink Lady)
bamboo skewers, soaked in water for 30 minutes

> ❝ The combination of sage and cayenne pepper provide an aromatic, flavoursome burst that packs a subtle punch. ❞

1 In a medium bowl, combine the salt, black pepper, dried sage, and cayenne pepper.

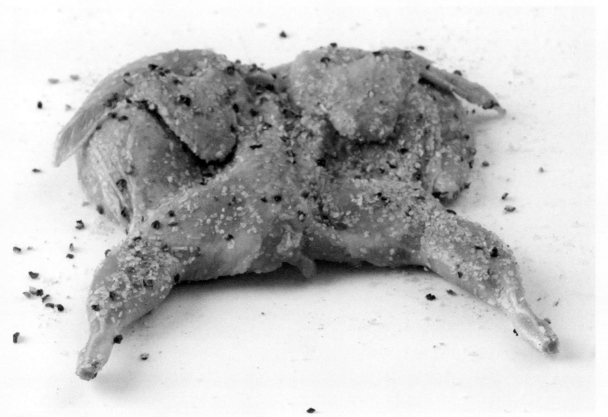

2 Cover the spatchcocked quails with an even amount of the rub, being certain to cover the cavities as well as the skin sides.

THE PREP

1 Halve the jalapeño peppers and remove their seeds, ribs, and stems.

2 Cut each tart apple into uniform slices.

3 Place 2 jalapeño halves and apple slices into the cavity of each quail.

4 Insert skewers into each quail to enclose the meat around the jalapeños and apples and to hold it tightly together.

5 Allow the quails to rest uncovered at room temperature for 45 minutes before going into the pit.

FEEL FREE TO USE OTHER FRUITS (SUCH AS PEACHES) IN PLACE OF THE APPLE SLICES.

))) THE SMOKE

1 With the pit temperature stabilized at 121°C (250°F), use tongs to place the quails in the middle of the pit and away from any hot spots.

2 After 45 minutes, test the quails for doneness by gently tugging downwards at the thigh to see if the legs separate from the body. (Avoid using an instant-read thermometer, as small birds have very little space for inserting it without touching bone.)

3 If the legs separate from the body, remove the quails from the smoker and allow to rest uncovered for 10 minutes.

SERVE EACH QUAIL HALVED TO ALLOW THE JALAPEÑOS AND APPLES TO EMERGE FROM THE CAVITY. THIS CREATES A STUNNING AND TEMPTING PRESENTATION.

Meat Poultry	**Wood** Hickory	**Prep time** 8¾ hrs	**Smoker temp** 121°C (250°F)	**Cook time** 1½ hrs	**Rest time** 10 mins	**Yield** Serves 3

On holiday, I once tasted a jerk seasoning that would have knocked my socks off, had I been wearing any. Its heat and complexity have inspired this recipe.

JERK-RUBBED CHICKEN WINGS

THE MEAT

12 very large chicken wing joints, each 85–115g (3–4oz), or bone-in thighs

• Very large chicken wings are sometimes sold jointed, as drumettes and middle joints.

• The tiny wing tip is most often removed, because it has no worthwhile meat.

• After being removed from the pit, chicken wings don't cook much further, due to their size and lack of significant bone mass.

THE FIRE

Light the pit fire 1 hour before smoking. Add wood 30 minutes before smoking.

• Target temp: 121°C (250°F)

• Wood needs: Low

TEMPERATURE GUIDE

	Cook time	Pull temp	Serving temp
Well	1½ hrs	79°C (175°F)	82°C (180°F)

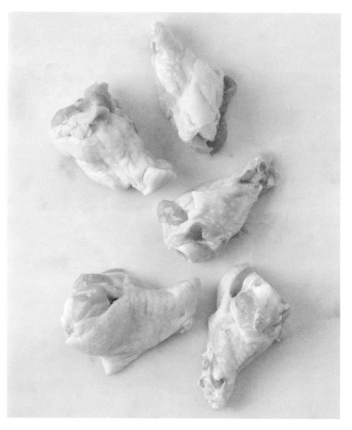

TIME PLAN (10 HRS 55 MINS)

30 mins	15 mins	8½ hrs	1½ hrs	10 mins
Build the fire	Make the rub	Rub and rest	Smoke	Rest

✳ THE RUB

Ingredients

1 tsp garlic powder
3 tsp cayenne pepper or habanero chilli powder
2 tsp onion powder
2 tsp dried thyme
2 tsp dried parsley
2 tsp granulated sugar
2 tsp salt
1 tsp paprika
1 tsp ground allspice
½ tsp freshly ground black pepper
½ tsp crushed chilli flakes
½ tsp ground nutmeg
¼ tsp ground cinnamon

START THE NIGHT BEFORE
The night before you plan to cook your wings is the best time to rub and rest them in the refrigerator. The jerk rub will then have a chance to deeply season the wings, creating an explosive bite.

1 In a medium bowl, thoroughly combine the garlic powder, cayenne pepper, onion powder, dried thyme, dried parsley, sugar, salt, paprika, allspice, black pepper, crushed chilli flakes, nutmeg, and cinnamon, until well mixed.

2 Place both the rub and the wings in a large zip-lock plastic food bag.

3 Close the bag and shake to coat the wings completely in the rub.

❝ I personally use habanero powder instead of cayenne pepper to kick up the heat on these wings. However, you can certainly take the amount of fire in your rub in whichever direction you like. ❞

4 Place the bag in the refrigerator overnight for a minimum of 8 hours. Remove the wings from the refrigerator for 30 minutes, to return to room temperature, before putting them into the pit.

〜 THE SMOKE

1 With the pit temperature stabilized at 121°C (250°F), use tongs to place the chicken wings in the middle of the pit, away from any hot spots.

2 After 1 hour, check the wings for doneness by pressing your finger to the meatiest part of each. It should feel firm and not have any elasticity when fully cooked. (You can pull some of meat away from bone to check as well.)

3 When the wings feel ready, after about 30 more minutes, remove them from the pit. Allow to rest uncovered for 10 minutes.

" Be sure to leave space between the chicken wings when placing them on the smoker. This allows air to circulate, ensuring the wings are cooked evenly. "

SERVE YOUR WINGS IN THE CENTRE OF THE TABLE, WITH SOME SLICED SPRING ONIONS, CELERY, AND LIME WEDGES (IF YOU'RE FEELING FANCY).

Meat
Poultry

Wood
Hickory

Prep time
45 mins

Smoker temp
121°C
(250°F)

Cook time
4½–5 hrs

Rest time
20 mins

Yield
Serves 3–4

A simply prepared whole chicken is a thing of beauty and a true comfort food. While smoking it is a bit challenging, this recipe will make your bird a real centrepiece.

WHOLE CHICKEN

THE MEAT

Whole chicken, 1.8–2.7kg (4–6lb)

• Look out for free-range chickens that fall within the weight range specified above. Avoid larger birds, as they tend to be older and so tougher; they will often not yield tender meat when smoked in the pit.

• While the smaller birds within the weight range specified seem to be more tender and take on smoke flavours more prominently, do not choose a bird smaller than this, as it may fall apart in the rigours of the firepit.

THE FIRE

Light the pit fire 1 hour before smoking. Add wood 30 minutes before smoking.

• Target temp: 121°C (250°F)

• Wood needs: Medium

TEMPERATURE GUIDE

	Cook time	Pull temp	Serving temp
Well	4½ hrs	74°C (165°F)	77°C (170°F)

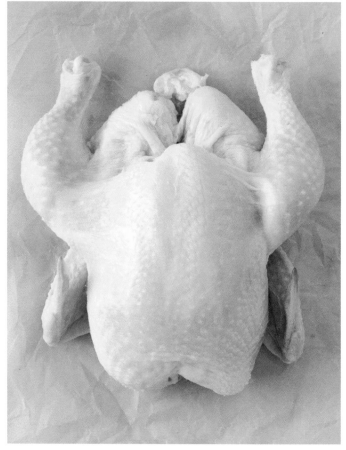

TIME PLAN (6 HRS 30 MINS TO 7 HRS)

30 mins	15 mins	30 mins	25 mins	4½–5 hrs	20 mins
Build the fire	Make the rub	Prep chicken	Rub and rest	Smoke	Rest

🖌 THE PREP

Ingredients

70g (2¼oz) coarse sea salt
100g (3½oz) light brown sugar
30g (1oz) cracked black pepper
1 tsp paprika
1 tsp ground cumin
1 tsp cayenne pepper
½ tsp dried sage
½ tsp dried thyme
3 garlic cloves, crushed or very finely chopped
4 5mm (¼in) thick slices of butter
1 lemon, cut into quarters

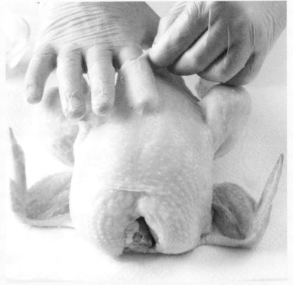

2 Release the skin from the breast meat by gently inserting your index finger under the skin and above the meat, making 2 pockets.

1 In a medium bowl, thoroughly mix the salt, light brown sugar, black pepper, paprika, cumin, cayenne pepper, sage, and thyme. Set aside.

FRESH OR FROZEN?

I prefer fresh chicken to a frozen bird. However, with frozen birds being reasonably priced, they've become an attractive option for cooks looking to serve large groups or to protect their wallets.

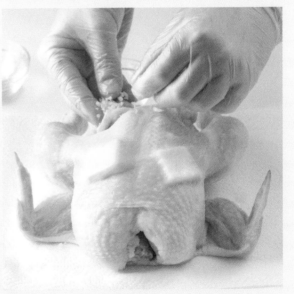

3 Gently stuff half the garlic and 2 slices of butter into each pocket.

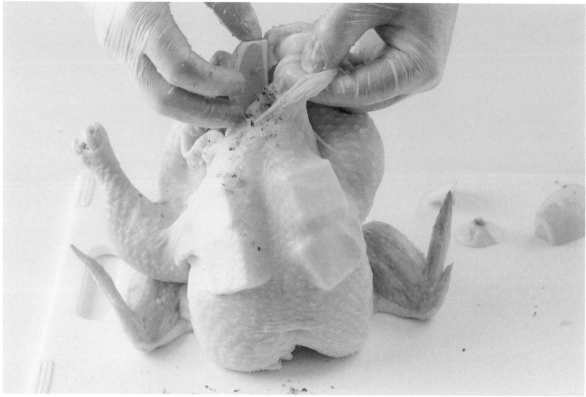

4 Place the lemon quarters into the cavity.

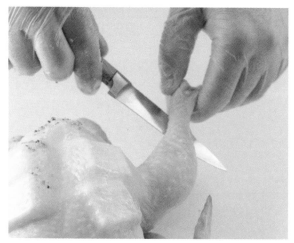

5 Using a sharp boning or paring knife, perform a quick truss of chicken legs: make a 2.5cm (1in) incision between tendon and bone, and push the opposite leg through to hold the chicken's shape.

6 Apply the rub evenly to the chicken, being sure to put some inside the cavity. Allow to rest uncovered for 25 minutes before going into the pit.

TRUSSING THE CHICKEN HELPS KEEP ITS SHAPE AND SO ALLOWS IT TO SMOKE MORE EVENLY.

〰 THE SMOKE

1 With the pit temperature stabilized at 121°C (250°F), place the chicken into the pit, making sure the cavity end faces the heat source and sits away from any hot spots.

2 After 3½ hours, insert an instant-read thermometer into the thickest part of the breast or thigh to check the progress, making sure the probe doesn't touch the bone. The target temperature for removing chicken is 74°C (165°F).

3 When it has reached the target temperature, after 1–1½ hours more, remove it from the pit. Allow to rest uncovered for 20 minutes.

4 Using a cleaver, chop the chicken into 8 evenly sized pieces: 2 drumsticks, 2 wings, 2 thighs, and 2 pieces of breast meat.

THE VERSATILITY OF SMOKED CHICKEN
A smoked chicken, prepared simply, is very versatile. You can pair it with everything from seasonal veggies to exotic sides, making it as simple or as sophisticated as you'd like.

SERVE WITH FRESH SEASONAL VEGETABLES AND ROASTED POTATOES FOR A DELIGHTFULLY DIFFERENT SUNDAY LUNCH.

134

Meat Poultry	**Wood** Hickory	**Prep time** 1½ hrs	**Smoker temp** 127°C (260°F)	**Cook time** 2½–3 hrs	**Rest time** 10 mins	**Yield** Serves 4

This rich, dark-meat chicken takes smoke remarkably well, and the addition of a mayonnaise-based sauce contributes a smack-your-lips tanginess.

CHICKEN THIGHS with PIQUANT MAYONNAISE

THE MEAT

8 skin-on bone-in chicken thighs, 1.35kg (3lb) in total

• Chicken thighs are the portion of the leg cut just above the knee joint.

• Their high fat and collagen content keep them moist at higher temperatures, unlike white-meat cuts, which can dry out during cooking.

• Buy thighs bone in and skin on; the skin adds a great protective layer to keep the meat moist.

🔥 THE FIRE

Light the pit fire 1 hour before smoking. Add wood 30 minutes before smoking.

• Target temp: 127°C (260°F)

• Wood needs: Low to medium

TEMPERATURE GUIDE

	Cook time	Pull temp	Serving temp
Well	2½–3 hrs	71°C to 74°C (160°F to 165°F)	77°C (170°F)

TIME PLAN (4 HRS 40 MINS TO 5 HRS 10 MINS)

30 mins	15 mins	45 mins	30 mins	2½–3 hrs	10 mins
Build the fire	Make the rub	Rub and rest	Make the sauce	Smoke	Rest

 THE RUB

Ingredients

140g (5oz) coarse sea salt
2 tbsp cracked black pepper or coarsely
    ground black pepper
1 tbsp granulated sugar
1 tsp cayenne pepper
1 tsp paprika
½ tsp dried sage
½ tsp dried thyme
120ml (4fl oz) extra virgin olive oil

**" If you want to kick up the heat a bit,
just add a little bit more cayenne pepper
to the rub; the rich mayonnaise sauce
will help to balance out the spice. "**

1 In a large bowl, combine the salt, black pepper, sugar, cayenne pepper, paprika, sage, and thyme.

2 Cover all sides of the chicken thighs with an even amount of rub. Pour the extra virgin olive oil in a small bowl and set aside.

3 Allow the chicken thighs to rest uncovered at room temperature, as below, for 45 minutes before going into the pit.

◖ THE SAUCE

Ingredients

300g (10oz) mayonnaise
240ml (8fl oz) white wine vinegar
75g (2½oz) horseradish sauce
1 tsp coarse sea salt
1 tsp cracked black pepper
¼ tsp cayenne pepper

1 In a large bowl, combine the mayonnaise, vinegar, horseradish sauce, salt, black pepper, and cayenne pepper.

2 Cover the bowl with cling film and refrigerate until ready for use.

ORIGIN OF THE SAUCE
This sauce – known in America as "Alabama white sauce" – is a unique regional barbecue creation that was developed in Decatur, Alabama, in 1925 by barbecue legend Big Bob Gibson. While it was originally developed for chicken and pork, it can be used on everything from all types of seafood to salads.

⟩⟩⟩ THE SMOKE

1 With the pit temperature stabilized at 127°C (260°F), use tongs to place the chicken thighs skin-side up in the middle of the pit, away from any hot spots.

2 After 1 hour, brush the skin side of the thighs with a light coating of extra virgin olive oil and flip each over.

3 After smoking for 1 more hour, flip the chicken thighs back over so they're skin-side up.

4 After smoking for 30 more minutes, insert an instant-read thermometer into a chicken thigh to check the progress, making sure it's not touching bone. The target temperature for removing chicken thighs is 71–74°C (160–165°F).

5 When the chicken thighs have reached the target temperature, up to 30 more minutes, remove them from the pit. Allow to rest uncovered for at least 10 minutes; they will continue to cook and reach the ideal serving temperature of 77°C (170°F).

6 Dip the chicken thighs into the sauce until they're coated before eating, if you like.

CHICKEN THIGHS ARE GREAT SERVED WITH SLICED PICKLES AND COLESLAW.

| Meat Poultry | Wood Oak | Prep time 2 hrs | Smoker temp 127°C (260°F) | Cook time 2 hrs 5 mins | Rest time 5 mins | Yield Serves 8 |

This recipe is a great opportunity to flex some culinary muscle and use your pit to smoke an otherwise traditionally grilled item. The resulting yakitori is a delicious and visually appealing dish that's well worth a bit of effort.

SMOKY YAKITORI CHICKEN

THE MEAT

24 very large chicken middle wing joints, about 85g (3oz) each, or bone-in thighs

• While you can buy frozen chicken wings, it's best to buy fresh wings. Look for those that are plump and meaty and have a good pink colour.

• This 3-part recipe involves cooking the yakitori chicken confit-style in smoky duck fat – it's cooked in hot fat but not deep-fried – and then sautéing to crisp the skin.

🔥 THE FIRE

Light the pit fire 1 hour before smoking. Add wood 30 minutes before smoking.

• Target temp: 127°C (260°F)

• Wood needs: Low to medium

TEMPERATURE GUIDE

	Cook time	Pull temp	Serving temp
Well	2 hrs 5 mins	74°C (165°F)	74°C (165°F)

TIME PLAN (4 HRS 10 MINS)

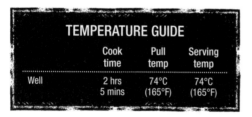

30 mins	30 mins	1 hr	30 mins	45 mins	45 mins	5 mins	5 mins
Build the fire	Make the sauce	Prep	Coat and rest	Smoke	Confit	Sauté	Rest

THE SAUCE

Ingredients

120ml (4fl oz) soy sauce
2 tbsp rice wine vinegar
1 tsp crushed garlic
1 tsp ground ginger
1 tsp granulated sugar
crushed chilli flakes, to taste

THE PREP

Ingredients

48 bamboo skewers longer than 15cm (6in),
    soaked in water for 30 minutes
coarse sea salt
freshly ground black pepper
1.75kg (3½lb) rendered duck fat

1 In a small bowl, whisk together the soy sauce, rice wine vinegar, crushed garlic, ground ginger, sugar, and crushed chilli flakes to taste.

2 Cover the bowl with cling film and refrigerate until ready for use.

> " Yakitori, which literally means 'grilled chicken', is a Japanese term used to refer to meats that are skewered and grilled. It is typically served as a fast food or street food, and is often eaten in Japan as a bar snack. "

1 Butterfly (open out) each chicken wing or thigh, and roughly flatten each piece into a fairly even rectangular shape, leaving the bones intact.

2 Using the tip of a boning knife, loosen the meat from the bones and roll each piece with your fingers to separate it a little from the flesh. Scrape the bones with the knife blade.

3 Insert 2 skewers into each chicken piece, perpendicular to the bones, just under the skin.

4 Season the chicken on all sides with a light coating of salt and black pepper.

5 Thoroughly coat each of the skewered wings in the yakitori sauce. Allow to rest uncovered at room temperature for at least 30 minutes before going into the pit.

))) THE SMOKE

1 Spoon the duck fat into a large saucepan and set aside, away from any open flames.

2 With the pit temperature stabilized at 127°C (260°F), use tongs to place the skewered chicken in the middle of the pit, skin-side up, and with even spacing between the pieces on all sides, as shown on the left.

3 Place the saucepan of duck fat onto a hot spot in the smoker.

IF YOU CAN STAND THE SKEWERS VERTICALLY WITH THE ENDS OUT OF THE FAT, YOU'LL HAVE AN EASIER TIME REMOVING THE CHICKEN.

4 After 45 minutes, carefully place the skewers into the smoky melted duck fat, making sure to submerge most of the meat in the fat.

5 After 45 more minutes, heat a large cast-iron frying pan on the barbecue, or a large sauté pan over a medium-high heat on the hob. Carefully transfer about 3 tbsp of the hot duck fat to the hot cast-iron frying pan or sauté pan. (The remaining fat can be used to roast potatoes.)

6 Working in batches, place the skewers, skin-side down, in the hot duck fat, and allow the skin to crisp up for 3–5 minutes before removing.

7 Allow the yakitori skewers to rest for at least 5 minutes before serving.

PRESENT THE YAKITORI ON A LARGE SERVING DISH, SPRINKLING WITH THINLY SLICED SPRING ONIONS AND A DRIZZLE OF THE YAKITORI SAUCE.

GAME

The tradition of smoking wild game stretches back across generations and cultures, and provides creative opportunities for more adventurous cooks. Whether you're an outdoors person with a passion for food, or a cook with a desire to step outside the normal range of meats, experimenting with game in a well-managed smoker can bring you unique – and delicious – results.

Meat	Wood	Prep time	Smoker temp	Cook time	Rest time	Yield
Venison	Apple	1¼ hrs	121°C (250°F)	40–50 mins	10 mins	Serves 4

The flavours in this recipe are a homage to the crisp autumn days of the deer hunting season. The grassy scent of sage and sweet, smoky apple are great with the rich, earthy taste of the tenderloin (sometimes sold as venison 'fillet').

VENISON TENDERLOIN

THE MEAT

2 whole venison tenderloins (fillets), 450g (1lb) each

• One of the leanest game cuts available, venison tenderloin has a deep flavour and is a great alternative to beef, pork, or poultry.

• The meat has less than 2 per cent fat and is very high in iron and B12 vitamins, making it a leaner and more nutritionally sound protein than some other, more fatty meats.

• The tenderloin is cut from the inside haunch of an adult deer and, like all tenderloins, is prized for its flavour and fine-grained texture.

SOURCING VENISON
Buying fresh venison might prove difficult in the supermarket. However, there are more and more online retailers who grow and sell meat from their own well-managed herds. This farmed venison is often more tender than the meat of a wild animal.

THE FIRE

Light the pit fire 1 hour before smoking. Add wood 30 minutes before smoking.

• Target temp: 121°C (250°F)
• Wood needs: Medium

TEMPERATURE GUIDE

	Cook time	Pull temp	Serving temp
Rare	40 mins	57°C (135°F)	60°C (140°F)
Medium rare	50 mins	58°C (136°F)	61°C (141°F)

THE PREP

Ingredients
bunch of fresh sage
1 apple (ideally a tart, crisp variety)
115g (4oz) unsalted butter

1 Divide the sage into 2 smaller bunches. (One will be used as a brush, while the other will be a garnish.) Set aside.

2 Slice the apple into 8 pieces. Set aside.

3 Place the butter in a medium flame- and ovenproof saucepan. Set aside.

" Experiment with different kinds of apples to see which varieties give the flavour you prefer. "

TIME PLAN (2 HRS 35 MINS TO 2 HRS 45 MINS)

30 mins	30 mins	15 mins	30 mins	40–50 mins	10 mins
Build the fire	Prep	Make the rub	Rub and rest	Smoke	Rest

 THE RUB

Ingredients

70g (2¼oz) coarse sea salt
30g (1oz) cracked black pepper
50g (1¾oz) granulated sugar
½ tbsp dried sage
1 tsp ground cumin
1 tsp paprika

1 In a medium bowl, combine the salt, black pepper, sugar, dried sage, cumin, and paprika.

2 Apply the rub liberally to all sides of the tenderloins.

3 Allow them to rest uncovered at room temperature for at least 30 minutes before going into the pit.

" You can cut back on – or add more of – any spice as you like in this rub. "

))) THE SMOKE

1 With the pit temperature stabilized at 121°C (250°F), use tongs to place the venison tenderloins in the middle of the pit, with the larger ends pointing towards the firebox, and away from any hot spots.

2 Place the pan of butter into the pit to melt.

3 After 15 minutes, dip the sage brush into the melted butter and paint it onto each tenderloin, as if you're basting.

4 After 20 more minutes, insert an instant-read thermometer into middle of each tenderloin to check the progress. The target temperature for removing tenderloins is 57°C (135°F) for rare meat.

5 Once the tenderloins have reached the target temperature, after 5–15 more minutes, paint on more butter with the sage brush and then remove from the pit. Allow the meat to rest for 10 minutes.

6 Meanwhile, slice the apple as directed and place the slices directly into the pit. Smoke for 5 minutes.

7 Slice the tenderloins into medallions and garnish with the smoked apple slices and some roughly chopped sage leaves.

Meat Pheasant	**Wood** Oak	**Prep time** 8½–12½ hrs	**Smoker temp** 104°C (220°F)	**Cook time** 4–4½ hrs	**Rest time** 10 mins	**Yield** Serves 4

Pheasant is often associated with the colours and sounds of autumn and the rustic smell of smoke. By allowing it to brine overnight before smoking, you can ensure this exquisite bird comes out of the smoker moist and delicious.

WHOLE PHEASANT

THE MEAT

Large whole pheasant, 1.1–1.35kg (2½–3lb)

- Pheasant is farmed meat, so you can now buy this delicious poultry in mainstream supermarkets as well as in speciality shops.

- For a change to this recipe, try making it with guinea fowl, a bird that is also increasingly widely available in larger supermarkets.

- Because it's a naturally lean protein, smoking pheasant can prove difficult. Let it cook too long and it will be dry, so watch your cooking time and the bird's internal temperature closely for the best results.

WHAT'S BRINING?
Brining is the process of soaking a protein in salted, sometimes seasoned water in order to add flavour and moisture. Brining is similar to the dry rub osmosis exchange, in that it will keep the pheasant tender and moist. While in the brine, the meat will absorb the salt water and sugar, deeply seasoning it.

THE FIRE

Light the pit fire 1 hour before smoking. Add wood 30 minutes before smoking.

- Target temp: 104°C (220°F)
- Wood needs: Medium

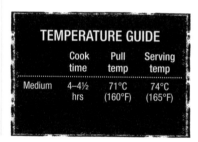

TEMPERATURE GUIDE

	Cook time	Pull temp	Serving temp
Medium	4–4½ hrs	71°C (160°F)	74°C (165°F)

THE BRINE

Ingredients
50g (1¾oz) light brown sugar
30g (1oz) coarse sea salt

1 In a large saucepan over a low heat, mix the sugar, salt, and 1.7–1.9 litres (3–3¼ pints) of warm water, stirring until the sugar and salt are dissolved. Remove from the heat and allow to cool completely.

2 Fully submerge the pheasant in the cold brine, cover with a lid, and refrigerate overnight.

3 Remove the pheasant from the refrigerator and pat it dry with kitchen paper.

❝ **The night before you plan to smoke the pheasant, make the brine, then soak the bird for 8–12 hours.** ❞

TIME PLAN (13 HRS 55 MINS TO 18 HRS 25 MINS)

30 mins	8½–12½ hrs	15 mins	30 mins	4–4½ hrs	10 mins
Build the fire	Prep	Make the rub	Rub and rest	Smoke	Sear

✳ THE RUB

Ingredients
50g (1¾oz) light brown sugar
1 tbsp dried sage
½ tbsp ground cumin
1 tsp garlic powder

1 In a medium bowl, combine the light brown sugar, dried sage, cumin, and garlic powder until well mixed.

2 Cover the entire surface of the pheasant with the rub. Allow the bird to rest uncovered at room temperature for 30 minutes before going into the pit.

3 Truss the pheasant by making a small incision in one leg between the ankle tendon and bone, and then threading through the opposite leg (see p130).

))) THE SMOKE

1 With the pit temperature stabilized at 104°C (220°F), use tongs to place the pheasant, breast side up, into the middle of the pit, with its cavity facing the heat source and away from any hot spots.

2 After 3½ hours, insert an instant-read thermometer into the side of a breast to check the progress. The target temperature for removing pheasant from the pit is 71°C (160°F).

3 Once the pheasant reaches the target temperature, after 30 minutes to 1 hour more, remove the bird from the pit. Allow it to rest uncovered for 10 minutes before carving; it will continue to cook and reach the ideal serving temperature of 74°C (165°F).

> " You don't have to limit pheasant to special occasions or holidays. It works well as an alternative to chicken in everyday cooking. "

Meat Wild boar	**Wood** Oak	**Prep time** 1 hr	**Smoker temp** 121°C (250°F)	**Cook time** 3½–4 hrs	**Rest time** 10 mins	**Yield** Serves 2

Wild boar ribs are lean yet relatively meaty cuts that have a rich, deep, and gamey flavour. They benefit from this simple seasoning that highlights the wild quality of the meat.

WILD BOAR RIBS

THE MEAT

1 rack of wild boar ribs, about 1.35kg (3lb)

• The rib section comes from the animal's side, just above the belly and below the loin.

• A small piece of the belly is often left intact on the rack of ribs, which is a great delicacy.

• The amount of intramuscular fat on wild boar ribs is much less than that found on a farmed animal.

THE FIRE

Light the pit fire 1 hour before smoking. Add wood 30 minutes before smoking.

• Target temp: 121°C (250°F)

• Wood needs: Medium

THE RUB

Ingredients

30g (1oz) coarse sea salt
30g (1oz) coarsely ground black pepper
1 tbsp light brown sugar
1 tbsp ground cumin

1 Combine the salt, black pepper, light brown sugar, and ground cumin.

2 Apply the rub liberally to all sides of the rib rack.

3 Allow it to rest uncovered at room temperature for at least 45 minutes before going into the pit.

THE SMOKE

1 With the pit temperature stabilized at 121°C (250°F), use tongs to place the rib rack into the middle of the pit and away from any hot spots.

2 After 3 hours, test the rack for doneness by lifting it in the middle of the rack with the tongs; it should feel flexible without cracking on surface. An instant-read thermometer is not a good gauge of doneness in this case, as there is so much bone that must be avoided.

3 Once the ribs have reached the target temperature and have a good flex, after 30 minutes to 1 hour more, remove them from the smoker. Allow to rest uncovered for 10 minutes before cutting into individual bones.

TEMPERATURE GUIDE

	Cook time	Pull temp	Serving temp
Well	3½–4 hrs	77°C (170°F)	82°C (180°F)

TIME PLAN (5 HRS 10 MINS TO 5 HRS 40 MINS)

30 mins	15 mins	45 mins	3 hrs 30 mins to 4 hrs	10 mins
Build the fire	Make the rub	Rub and rest	Smoke	Rest

Meat
Bison

Wood
Oak

Prep time
1 hr

Smoker temp
135°C
(275°F)

Cook time
40 mins

Rest time
10 mins

Yield
Serves 2

An interesting meat and a curiosity that is well worth seeking out online and in farmer's markets. Its deep maroon colour makes it visually stunning.

BISON RIBEYE

THE MEAT

2 bison ribeye steaks, about 225g (8oz) each

• Bison ribeye is typically sold off the bone; a good thing for consumers paying by weight, considering the size of the back rib bones.

• This little-used loin muscle contains considerably less fat marbling than its beef cousin, but is still tender and full of flavour.

THE FIRE

Light the pit fire 1 hour before smoking. Add wood 30 minutes before smoking.

• Target temp: 135°C (275°F)

• Wood needs: Low

TEMPERATURE GUIDE

	Cook time	Pull temp	Serving temp
Rare	40 mins	57°C (135°F)	60°C (140°F)

✸ THE RUB

Ingredients

140g (5oz) coarse sea salt
115g (4oz) coarsely ground black pepper

1 Place the steaks on a shallow tray. Apply a liberal amount of salt and black pepper to each side, massaging the seasonings into meat, then coat the edges, too.

2 Allow them to rest uncovered at room temperature for at least 45 minutes before going into the pit.

❝ I use the 'reverse sear' method when preparing bison ribeye steaks (see p46). You can place the steaks in a hot cast-iron pan or lay them directly on the coals of a charcoal grill for a quick sear finish. ❞

⑅ THE SMOKE

1 With the pit temperature stabilized at 135°C (275°F), use tongs to place the steaks into the middle of the pit.

2 After 30 minutes, insert an instant-read thermometer into the middle of the steaks to check the progress. Target temperature for removing bison ribeye is 57°C (135°F).

3 Once the steaks reach the target temperature, about 10 more minutes, remove from the smoker and transfer immediately to the coals or a hot cast-iron pan. Sear for 2 minutes per side.

4 Remove the steaks from the coals or pan. Allow them to rest uncovered for 10 minutes before serving.

TIME PLAN (2½ HRS)

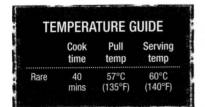

30 mins	15 mins	45 mins	40 mins	10 mins	10 mins
Build the fire	Make the rub	Rub and rest	Smoke	Sear	Rest

Meat Elk	**Wood** Oak or apple	**Prep time** 1 hr	**Smoker temp** 141°C (285°F)	**Cook time** 50 mins to 1½ hrs	**Rest time** 10 mins	**Yield** Serves 8

An elk fillet – meat which is farmed in the UK and available online – is a lean and tender cut that takes smoke flavours very well. However, be very careful to remove it from the heat when it reaches target temperature, so it doesn't overcook.

ELK FILLET

THE MEAT

Elk fillet (tenderloin), about 1.35kg (3lb)

• The fillet (sometimes sold as tenderloin) is cut from the back of the animal, just below the spine.

• A muscle that's very lightly used, fillet is lean and not nearly as marbled as ribeye.

• This cut should be cooked pretty rare to medium at most and served as medallions. If your preference is for more well-done meat, this may not be the best choice for you.

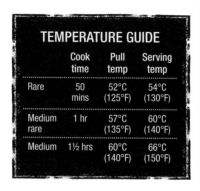

TEMPERATURE GUIDE			
	Cook time	Pull temp	Serving temp
Rare	50 mins	52°C (125°F)	54°C (130°F)
Medium rare	1 hr	57°C (135°F)	60°C (140°F)
Medium	1½ hrs	60°C (140°F)	66°C (150°F)

THE FIRE

Light the pit fire 1 hour before smoking. Add wood 30 minutes before smoking.

• Target temp: 141°C (285°F)

• Wood needs: Low

 THE RUB

Ingredients

30g (1oz) coarse sea salt
30g (1oz) cracked black pepper
1 tbsp granulated sugar

1 Pat the elk fillet dry with pieces of kitchen paper.

2 In a medium bowl, combine the salt, black pepper, and sugar. Apply this rub all over each surface of the fillet.

3 Allow it to rest uncovered at room temperature for 45 minutes before going into the pit.

THE SMOKE

1 With the pit temperature stabilized at 141°C (285°F), use tongs to place the meat in an area closest to the firebox or another hot spot.

2 After 50 minutes, insert an instant-read thermometer into the fillet to check the progress of the meat.

3 Once the fillet has reached your preferred temperature, after up to 30 more minutes, remove it from the pit. Allow it to rest uncovered for 10 minutes before slicing.

❝ **Try to minimize the number of times you insert the probe. Numerous holes allow juices to escape.** ❞

TIME PLAN (2½ HRS TO 3 HRS 10 MINS)

30 mins	15 mins	45 mins	50 mins to 1½ hrs	10 mins
Build the fire	Make the rub	Rub and rest	Smoke	Rest

SERVE THE ELK WITH ROAST OR SMOKED GARLIC BULBS AND STREW THE MEAT WITH SPRIGS OF THYME

A LITTLE EXTRA SMOKE

While your smoker can successfully help you prepare all sorts of delicious smoked meat, you don't have to stop there. The delicate taste of trout, the salty brine of an oyster, and the bold fattiness of salmon all benefit from the intense flavours that smoke brings. From smoked mushroom caps to smoked habanero hot sauce, you can develop new layers of flavour and sweetness in vegetables, all in the warm embrace of your smoker pit.

SMOKING SEAFOOD: WHAT YOU NEED to KNOW

Modern transportation methods have made finding and buying top-quality fresh fish and shellfish easier than ever. Because of this, the available options for what you can smoke are broad and exciting, and these tips and tricks will help you create amazingly delicious seafood on the smoker.

IN THE KITCHEN

Preparing seafood for the smoker starts with observing some simple but important safety rules and following a few simple prep tips.

Safety should always be a top priority

Use fresh fish immediately to minimize potential safety issues. When storing uncooked seafood in the refrigerator, place it on ice and smoke it within 2 days of purchasing. Although using frozen seafood isn't ideal, if you do plan to freeze uncooked seafood then wrap it tightly in freezer bags and freeze it immediately. Frozen seafood should be smoked within 3 months of freezing, or discarded. Properly refrigerate or freeze any leftovers, and don't let them stay too long in storage. Discard uneaten, refrigerated leftovers after a few days.

As a general rule, don't remove the skin

Some fish recipes require you to remove the skin, whereas others retain the skin to trap in heat and flavour. Keeping the skin intact also makes it easier to keep the fish intact as you handle it on the smoker. If you need to remove the skin, you can do so yourself, or ask the fishmonger to do it for you.

Always remove bones from fish

One key aspect to cooking fish that doesn't change, regardless of method, is removing the bones, especially the tiny "pin bones". Invest in a pair of needle-nosed pliers for removing small bones, and become familiar with where little pin bones might hide within a fish's flesh (usually centrally on fillets, on either side of where the spine once was).

PURCHASE QUALITY CUTS

Use your senses when buying fish.

GRADE	SMOKE QUALITY	DESCRIPTION
Fresh from a good fishmonger	Excellent	Any fresh seafood that has not been long off the boat is usually of top quality, with good flavour, freshness, and scent. Always try to buy fish and seafood that has been sourced sustainably; a good fishmonger should be able to tell you about their sources.
Supermarket fish	Poor	Fish and seafood from a supermarket is a hit-and-miss affair. Read packaging carefully to check it has not been previously frozen and then thawed. Any fish that smells 'fishy' should be avoided.

Marinades and rubs can bring out unique and hidden flavours

Unless you're going to cold smoke salmon, most seafood won't benefit from brining. Experiment with soy sauce marinades, or create your own concoctions, but use seasonings carefully as they can easily overwhelm the delicate flavours of milder fish and seafood. More powerful seasonings such as sage or rosemary complement salmon beautifully, but more subtly flavoured fish might be overwhelmed.

Use the smell test

While it seems strange to say, fish shouldn't have a fishy smell or a lingering ammonia odour, both of which can be signs that bacteria have begun to deteriorate the flesh and indicate the fish may be past its prime. Fresh fish should actually smell like clean water or the ocean. Any fish that has a fishy or lingering ammonia odour should be discarded immediately, no matter how recently it was purchased, or how fresh it may appear to the eye.

ON THE SMOKER

Things happen quickly when you're smoking seafood, but following these simple guidelines will ensure that it smokes beautifully.

Elevate flavours with your wood choices

Oak is a good wood for beginner smokers because it doesn't burn quickly but does burn efficiently. It imparts a mild flavour and gives fish a beautiful reddish colour. As you become a more experienced smoker, you can test other woods – such as pecan, apple, and hickory – with a small cut of fish and learn what flavour dynamics those woods impart.

Learning how a wood burns, how fast it burns, how it smells when burned, and what flavours it imparts to a particular fish, will go a long way towards helping you become a better smoker.

Seafood smokes really quickly

Because seafood cooks quickly, you'll have to remain focused on your fire and your smoker's temperature. You can't just put the food in your smoker and come back a few hours later. Smoking seafood requires constant monitoring.

Don't allow fish to linger in your smoker

It's vital to remove fish from the smoker before it looks completely finished. Residual heat trapped in the flesh will finish the cooking process, and removing it from the smoker promptly will result in food that's moist and tasty, not rubbery and bland.

Learn to gauge doneness

Smoking seafood takes very little time, less than 1 hour in most cases. This means it's easy to gauge doneness by observing these guidelines:
• Fish fillets will flake easily.
• Lobster, oysters, and shrimp will become firm and opaque.
• Whole fish will show flaking around the gills and the stomach incision.

Shorter cooking times for fish and seafood require good meal planning

Because seafood smokes quickly, it's important to have other items you're serving with it ready to go by the time your fish comes off the smoker. Everyone loves to enjoy a hot meal, but if your salmon is hot and your green beans are cold, you'll have unhappy eaters.

Try seasoned wood chips

If you wish to enhance – but not challenge – the flavour offered by the wood with which you smoke fish, consider soaking wood chips in water mixed with garlic powder or onion powder. You can then add these wood chips to your fire as needed to keep the smoker temperature at a constant level and to provide just a hint of additional seasoning.

| **Meat** Seafood | **Wood** Oak | **Prep time** 40 mins | **Smoker temp** 121°C (250°F) | **Cook time** 45 mins | **Rest time** 10 mins | **Yield** Serves 8 |

Whole smoked fish, especially a delicate fish such as rainbow trout, take the flavours from the smoke of a hardwood – oak, in this case – exceptionally well.

WHOLE RAINBOW TROUT

THE FISH

8 whole rainbow trout, skin on, bone out, about 675g (1½lb) each

• You can choose between 2 types of trout: wild and farmed.

• Buying fresh, not frozen, fish – as well as leaving the head and tail intact and the skin on – keeps in moisture during the cooking process.

• While having the bones removed is convenient, it's not necessary. But don't try it yourself unless you're an expert; ask the fishmonger to do it.

🔥 THE FIRE

Light the pit fire 1 hour before smoking. Add wood 30 minutes before smoking.

• Target temp: 121°C (250°F)

• Wood needs: Low

> **A low fire with a strong base of coals will allow you to impart plenty of smoke flavour.**

❊ THE RUB

Ingredients

70g (2¼oz) coarse sea salt
50g (1¾oz) granulated sugar
1 tbsp freshly ground white pepper
1 tsp ground coriander
1 tsp ground cumin
1 tsp cayenne pepper
½ tsp paprika
225g (8oz) unsalted butter, melted
2 lemons, quartered

1 In a medium bowl, thoroughly mix the salt, sugar, white pepper, coriander, cumin, cayenne pepper, and paprika. Set aside.

2 Place the trout in a large pan. Pour the butter over the fish, coating all surfaces and cavities.

3 Evenly cover the trout inside and out with the rub. Insert a lemon quarter inside each fish.

4 Allow to rest for 25 minutes before going into the pit.

〰 THE SMOKE

1 With your pit temperature stabilized at 121°C (250°F), place the trout directly on the racks in the middle of the pit and away from any hot spots.

2 After 30 minutes, gently roll the trout onto their other sides. Check the firmness of the flesh: carefully lift the skin at the edge of the gills and poke the flesh gently with a finger or fork. It should feel firm, not spongey.

3 After 15 more minutes, check the firmness of the flesh again. When the fish flakes easily near the body cavity opening, remove it from the pit.

4 Allow to rest uncovered for 10 minutes before serving.

TIME PLAN (2 HRS 5 MINS)

30 mins	15 mins	25 mins	45 mins	10 mins
Build the fire	Make the rub	Rub and rest	Smoke	Rest

Meat Seafood	**Wood** Oak	**Prep time** 1 hr 20 mins	**Smoker temp** 121°C (250°F)	**Cook time** 50 mins to 1 hr	**Rest time** 10 mins	**Yield** Serves 4

Red snapper is an exotic fish, available online and at good fishmongers; substitute native red mullet if you prefer. Both have a vibrant colour. Their meaty flesh adapts well to smoking and is versatile: Asian flavours work just as well as barbecue sauce or herbs.

RED SNAPPER

THE FISH

2 whole red snapper, about 1.8–2.7kg (4–6lb) each

• Red snapper is a reef-dwelling fish native to the western Atlantic Ocean and the Gulf of Mexico; red mullet is found in warmer UK waters.

• A whole red snapper will feed 2 people; red mullet are smaller fish and you willl need 1 for each diner.

• It is best to cook both red snapper and red mullet with the skin on, to preserve moisture and hold in the natural saline flavours.

THE FIRE

Light the pit fire 1 hour before smoking. Add wood 30 minutes before smoking.

• Target temp: 121°C (250°F)
• Wood needs: Low

THE RUB

Ingredients

4 tbsp coarse sea salt
2 tsp smoked paprika
2 tsp light brown sugar
2 tsp ground cumin
1 tsp garlic powder
1–2 tsp cayenne pepper
225g (8oz) unsalted butter
2 lemons, sliced into wedges
bunch of fresh coriander, roughly chopped

1 In a medium bowl, combine the salt, smoked paprika, brown sugar, cumin, garlic powder, and cayenne pepper, and mix thoroughly. Set aside.

2 Melt the unsalted butter in a large, wide sauté pan.

3 With a sharp knife, score the outside of each fish with 2 shallow, angled cuts on each side.

4 Place the fish into the pan and coat it with melted butter, being sure it gets into the cavities of each fish. Liberally sprinkle the rub inside and out.

5 Divide the lemons and three-quarters of the coriander between each cavity.

6 Allow to rest uncovered at room temperature for 35 minutes before going into the pit.

WHEN YOU BUY
Ask that the heads be left on, but that the scales and dorsal fins be removed. Scaling is time-consuming and dorsal fins have spines that can prick your fingers.

TIME PLAN (2 HRS 50 MINS TO 3 HRS)

30 mins	15 mins	30 mins	35 mins	50 mins to 1 hr	10 mins
Build the fire	Make the rub	Prep	Rub and rest	Smoke	Rest

))) THE SMOKE

1 With your pit temperature stabilized at 121°C (250°F), use tongs to place the red snapper in the middle of the pit, heads facing the heat source.

2 After 30 minutes, carefully turn over the fish and insert an instant-read thermometer just behind the gills, in the thickest part of each. The target temperature for removing red snapper is 66°C (150°F).

3 Once the red snapper just passes the temperature, after 20–30 more minutes, remove it from the pit.

4 Allow the red snapper to rest uncovered for 10 minutes; it will continue to cook and reach the ideal serving temperature of 68°C (155°F). Serve with the reserved coriander.

" **When you garnish the fish with more coriander, the fresh, aromatic herb complements the sweet and smoky flavour of the snapper. You can also serve it with jalapeño peppers, even barbecue sauce for dipping.** "

Meat Seafood	**Wood** Oak	**Prep time** 1 hr 5 mins	**Smoker temp** 121°C (250°F)	**Cook time** 45 mins	**Rest time** 5 mins	**Yield** Serves 4

The cooking time here is just enough to impart a mild smoke that is complemented by a sweet glaze; both balance the salmon well.

SALMON with SWEET GLAZE

THE FISH

4 salmon fillets, skin on 1 side, 115–175g (4–6oz) each

• Once you master this recipe, try smoking whole sides of salmon for a truly celebratory dish.

• Look for farmed organic salmon, or wild fish if you want to splash out.

• Fresh fish shouldn't smell fishy, but instead have a mild scent of the sea.

THE FIRE

Light the pit fire 1 hour before smoking. Add wood 30 minutes before smoking.

• Target temp: 121°C (250°F)

• Wood needs: Low

❝ **If you prefer your salmon to be skinless, your fishmonger will be happy to remove the skin from the fillets for you.** ❞

THE RUB

Ingredients

2 tbsp coarse sea salt
2 tbsp freshly ground black pepper

1 Season the salmon all over with the salt and black pepper.

2 Allow it to rest uncovered at room temperature for 30 minutes before going into the pit.

THE GLAZE

Ingredients

75g (2½oz) honey
1 tbsp olive oil
pinch of crushed chilli flakes
1 garlic clove, crushed or finely chopped

1 In a heavy-based flame- and ovenproof saucepan, combine the honey, olive oil, crushed chilli flakes, and garlic. Set aside.

THE SMOKE

1 With the pit temperature stabilized at 121°C (250°F), carefully place the fish fillets directly on the middle rack.

2 Place the saucepan of glaze into the pit to allow it to warm up and take on some of its own mild smoke flavour.

3 After 15 minutes, use a brush to quickly and gently paint a thin layer of glaze across the top of each salmon fillet. Repeat after 15 more minutes.

4 After 10 further minutes, check the doneness of the fish by testing whether it flakes easily to the touch. When they are ready, about 5 more minutes, brush once more with the glaze and remove from the pit.

5 Allow to rest uncovered for 5 minutes before serving.

TIME PLAN (2 HRS 25 MINS)

30 mins	15 mins	30 mins	20 mins	45 mins	5 mins
Build the fire	Make the rub	Rub and rest	Make the glaze	Smoke	Rest

GARNISH THE SALMON WITH SALTED, CHILLI-DUSTED LIMES. THE CITRUS WILL HELP BALANCE THE SWEET FLAVOURS AND WONDERFULLY COMPLEMENT THE FISH.

Meat
Seafood

Wood
Oak

Prep time
3 days 20 mins

Smoker temp
71°C
(160°F)

Cook time
1 hr

Rest time
1 hr

Yield
6–8

This recipe includes a brine-curing process, adding cold smoking to create a unique texture and flavour for a new kind of barbecue tradition.

COLD-SMOKED SALMON

 ### THE FISH

Whole salmon side, skin on, about 1kg (2¼lb)

• Whole salmon sides are readily available in supermarkets and fishmongers. For a special occasion, seek out farmed organic or wild fish

• Look for whole sides that have an even, meaty appearance.

• Because salmon is high in fat and moisture content, a whole side with a bit of belly fat on the lower portion can withstand the intensive curing and smoking processes here.

 ### THE FIRE

Light the pit fire 1 hour before smoking. Add wood 30 minutes before smoking.

• Evenly distribute coals throughout the firebox to disperse the heat. Just before placing the salmon in the pit, add additional fresh wood to the coals and then shut off the vents to the firebox to produce a smouldering fire.

• Target temp: 71°C (160°F)

• Wood needs: Low

THE RUB

Ingredients

420g (15oz) coarse sea salt
400g (14oz) granulated sugar
225g (8oz) cracked black pepper
400g (14oz) light brown sugar
4 large jalapeño peppers, sliced into thin rings

1 In a medium bowl, mix the salt, granulated sugar, black pepper, and light brown sugar.

2 Place the salmon skin side down in a large, non-reactive dish (glass or ceramic, not metal) twice as deep as the thickest part of the fish.

3 Cover the salmon evenly with the curing rub and jalapeño pepper rings. Cover and store in the refrigerator for 3 days.

WHAT'S BRINE CURING?
Brine curing is the process of preserving fish using a salt solution. It's a culinary tradition that goes back to before the Middle Ages, when fishermen would salt and bury fish to preserve them. Since then, curing salmon has become part of many cultural traditions, from Scandinavian cultures (where it's known as *gravlax*) to Jewish cuisine (where it's called *lox*).

TIME PLAN (3 DAYS 2 HRS 40 MINS)

3 days	20 mins	30 mins	1 hr	1 hr
Brine curing	Prep	Build the fire	Smoke	Rest

🔪 THE PREP

1 Remove the salmon from the cure and gently rinse under cold water to remove any remaining pockets of salt and sugar. The fish should have a firmer texture and look much darker in colour than it did before the curing process.

2 Fill a large saucepan or roasting tin with ice. Place a rack on top of the ice.

3 Place the salmon skin-side down on the rack above the ice, making sure the flesh does not touch the ice.

PLAN AHEAD!
Brine curing is critical to the success of this recipe. Give the salmon a full 3 days to cure in the refrigerator before you put it on the smoker.

A LITTLE BIT OF SCIENCE
Don't worry about covering the skin side of the salmon when putting on the brine-curing rub. The dry ingredients will liquefy via the osmosis process, forming a brine that will work its way into the fish.

🔥 THE SMOKE

1 After making sure the ventilation is shut off to the cooking chamber of the smoker, carefully place the ice pan with its rack and the fish in the coolest part of the pit.

2 Cold-smoke the salmon at or below 71°C (160°F) for 1 hour. The ice will melt, but the evaporating water means that the temperature surrounding the fish will stay cool.

3 After 1 hour, carefully remove the salmon from the pit and refrigerate uncovered for 1 hour.

4 Using a sharp knife, slice the salmon into thin strips.

Meat
Seafood

 Wood
Oak

 Prep time
50 mins

 Smoker temp
121°C
(250°F)

 Cook time
20 mins

 Rest time
5 mins

 Yield
Serves 4

These prawn skewers are great to pop in when you're smoking larger cuts of meat with longer cooking times. Put them in the pit for a great snack to enjoy while you and your guests await the slower-cooked items.

PRAWN SKEWERS

 THE FISH

1kg (2¼lb) very large jumbo king prawns, tails on, peeled and deveined

• Buying prawns fresh is always the ideal; however, the vast majority on sale are flash-frozen and these are fine to use.

• Look out for giant prawns for this recipe – order them from a good fishmonger – to give a real wow factor to the skewers.

• Be sure to buy prawns with the tails left on. The tails make great handles for picking up the prawns. You can ask the fishmonger to peel and devein them for you, if you prefer.

 THE FIRE

Light the pit fire 1 hour before smoking. Add wood 30 minutes before smoking.

• Target temp: 121°C (250°F)

• Wood needs: Low

CHOOSING PRAWNS
There are a few environmental concerns surrounding some farmed prawns. Buying your seafood from a reputable fishmonger – and asking them where their prawns come from and how they were farmed – should settle any anxieties.

TIME PLAN (1¾ HRS)

30 mins	20 mins	15 mins	15 mins	20 mins	5 mins
Build the fire	Prep	Make the rub	Rub and rest	Smoke	Rest

HOW TO DEVEIN PRAWNS

1 Gently pull the shell from each prawn, leaving the tail intact.

2 With a sharp knife, cut along the back of each prawn, being careful not to cut too deep.

3 Use the edge of the knife to pull out the dark thread-like vein. Discard it.

THE PREP

1 If your prawns are frozen, place them in a large bowl and run cool water over them until each piece feels thawed. (This can take up to 1 hour, depending on the number of prawns.)

2 Once the prawns have thawed, pat them dry with a piece of kitchen paper.

3 Soak 10–12 long bamboo skewers in water for about 30 minutes.

> **If your prawns are fresh, simply rinse them under cool water, and then pat each of them dry with kitchen paper.**

THE RUB

Ingredients

1½ tbsp coarse sea salt
1½ tsp freshly ground black pepper
1 tsp cayenne pepper
1 tsp garlic powder

1 In a medium bowl, combine the salt, black pepper, cayenne pepper, and garlic powder.

2 Toss the prawns in the rub, applying a light but even coating to each one.

3 Divide the prawns evenly between the skewers, piercing them in the middle and leaving spaces between each.

4 Allow the prawns to rest uncovered for 15 minutes before going into the pit.

THE SMOKE

1 With the pit temperature stabilized at 121°C (250°F), use tongs to place the prawn skewers in the middle of the pit and away from any hot spots.

2 After 15 minutes, check the prawns for doneness. They should feel firm to the touch throughout and have an opaque light pink colour.

3 When ready, after about 5 more minutes, remove the prawns from the pit. Allow them to rest uncovered for 5 minutes before serving.

I LIKE TO SERVE PRAWN SKEWERS IN THE CENTRE OF THE TABLE WITH A DISH OF GARLIC BUTTER OR HOT SAUCE.

Meat Seafood	**Wood** Oak	**Prep time** 35 mins	**Smoker temp** 121°C (250°F)	**Cook time** 15 mins	**Rest time** None	**Yield** Serves 6–8

While oysters may seem like an unusual choice for the smoker treatment, these sweet, tender, and briny bivalves take on smoke very well due to the liquor in their shells. Here, they're paired with a simple vinaigrette that enhances their natural salinity.

OYSTERS

THE SEAFOOD

24 large oysters

- If you prefer not to shuck the oysters yourself, be sure to have the fishmonger reserve the liquor, as well as provide 24 half-shells for cooking the oysters in.

- If you shuck the oysters yourself, be sure to use a stout oyster knife and hold the oyster with a towel to protect your hand.

- In years past, many recommended oysters be eaten in colder months due to inadequate refrigeration for transport in warmer months. These days, however, it's considered safe to eat oysters year-round.

THE FIRE

Light the pit fire 1 hour before smoking. Add wood 30 minutes before smoking.

- Target temp: 121°C (250°F)
- Wood needs: Low

OYSTERS: NOT ALL THE SAME
Depending on what part of the world you're in, the taste, size, and texture of oysters can vary significantly. Where oysters are harvested and how they're grown results in flavours that vary from savoury to sweet, and textures that can range from creamy to crunchy.

TIME PLAN (1 HR 20 MINS)

30 mins	15 mins	20 mins	15 mins
Build the fire	Make the sauce	Prep	Smoke

HOW TO SHUCK OYSTERS

The following are some basic steps for preparing the oysters on your own:

1 Be sure to tap the shells of oysters to ensure they close up. Discard any that don't shut.

2 Using a stiff-bristled brush, scrub any grit or dirt from the outside of the shells.

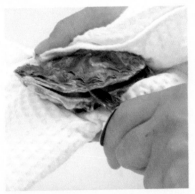

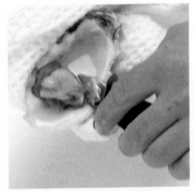

3 Holding each oyster in a thick towel, use an oyster knife to carefully pry open the shell, reserving the liquor inside.

4 Separate the oyster from its shell with the knife, leaving it inside.

THE SAUCE

Ingredients

½ red onion, very finely chopped
1 garlic clove, crushed or very finely chopped
1 tsp sea salt
1 tsp freshly ground white pepper
2 tbsp white wine vinegar
240ml (8fl oz) extra virgin olive oil

1 In a jar with a tight-fitting lid, place the red onion, garlic, salt, white pepper, white wine vinegar, and extra virgin olive oil.

2 Seal the jar tightly and shake it well to mix the ingredients until they emulsify. Set aside.

THE PREP

1 Assemble the oysters by placing 1 oyster and a bit of its liquor into a half shell.

2 Shake the jar to re-emulsify the sauce, then spoon a small amount of sauce into each oyster.

" **I like to serve smoked oysters with another splash of the vinaigrette and a crusty French baguette or other rustic bread. This makes a great vehicle for mopping up all the sauce left in the serving plate and also complements the texture of the oysters. This is a great dish for pairing with crisp, chilled white wine.** "

THE SMOKE

1 With the pit temperature stabilized at 121°C (250°F), add another log to the fire and close all the vents. The goal is to create a heavy smoke, filling the cooking chamber.

2 Use tongs to place the oyster shells in the middle of the pit, ensuring you keep a space between each.

3 After 15 minutes, check the oysters for doneness. They are ready when the flesh has turned opaque and the liquor has taken on a sooty colour.

4 When the oysters are done, remove to a serving tray and serve immediately.

Meat Seafood	**Wood** Pecan	**Prep time** 35 mins	**Smoker temp** 121°C (250°F)	**Cook time** 40 mins	**Rest time** 5 mins	**Yield** Serves 4

Lobster tails offer a more manageable and affordable cooking choice than whole lobsters. This recipe adds a garlic-chilli butter to enhance the smoked flavours.

LOBSTER TAIL

THE SEAFOOD

4 large lobster tails, shells intact, each 450g (1lb)

• Ask where your lobster tails come from before you buy. Cold-water lobster tails are more consistent in size and flavour than warm-water lobster tails. Also, cold-water lobster tails are firmer and sweeter.

• Lobster can be expensive, and by discarding only the shell surrounding the meat after you've eaten the tails, you have less waste than if you had bought a whole lobster.

THE FIRE

Light the pit fire 1 hour before smoking. Add wood 30 minutes before smoking.

• Target temp: 121°C (250°F)

• Wood needs: Low

THE PREP

1 Using kitchen shears, cut the underside of each lobster tail section lengthways.

2 Insert a 20cm (8in) skewer into each tail along the ridge at the top of the shell. This will keep the tails from curling up during smoking. Set aside.

THE SAUCE

Ingredients

1 tsp finely grated orange zest
½ tsp cayenne pepper
1 garlic clove, crushed
60g (2oz) unsalted butter

1 Once the pit temperature has reached 121°C (250°F), place a heavy-based flame- and ovenproof saucepan on the pit.

2 Add the orange zest, cayenne pepper, garlic, and butter, and stir until the butter melts.

THE SMOKE

1 With the pit temperature stabilized at 121°C (250°F), add another log to the fire and close all the vents. Use tongs to place the lobster tails, cut-sides up, into the middle of the pit and away from any hot spots.

2 After 15 minutes, working quickly, brush some of the sauce onto each tail. Repeat this process at the 30-minute mark.

3 After 15 more minutes, test the lobster tails for doneness. They are ready when the meat is firm and appears white and opaque throughout.

4 When done, remove the tails from the pit and allow to rest uncovered for at least 5 minutes.

TIME PLAN (1 HR 50 MINS)

30 mins	15 mins	20 mins	40 mins	5 mins
Build the fire	Prep	Make the sauce	Smoke	Rest

SERVE WITH THE REMAINING SMOKED GARLIC-CHILLI BUTTER AND GRILLED LEMON AND ARTICHOKE WEDGES.

Side Mushroom	**Wood** Oak	**Prep time** 8½–12½ hrs	**Smoker temp** 121°C (250°F)	**Cook time** 30 mins	**Rest time** 5 mins	**Yield** Serves 4

Portobello mushroom caps make a great smoked side dish, or even a main dish for any herbivores that may wander inadvertently into your meat-loving home.

SMOKED PORTOBELLO MUSHROOM CAPS

THE SIDE

4 large portobello mushrooms

• Large portobello mushrooms are fairly common in most supermarkets. Select those that are of a uniform size and firm to the touch.

• Portobello mushrooms have gills – feathery brown lines – on the underside. You can scrape them out with a spoon, but removing them is purely optional.

• To remove the stems from the mushrooms, simply hold a mushroom in your hand and twist the stem gently at the base with the other hand. The stems can be used for stock or soup.

A GREAT OPTION FOR SMOKING
Meaty and thick portobellos are excellent for the smoker, as they're less likely to fall apart when marinating and smoking.

THE FIRE

Light the pit fire 1 hour before smoking. Add wood 30 minutes before smoking.

• Target temp: 121°C (250°F)
• Wood needs: Low

THE PREP

1 Remove the stems from the mushroom caps and scrape out the gills, if you prefer (see left).

2 Using kitchen paper or a pastry brush, gently brush any loose dirt from the outside of each cap (but don't rinse them).

THE MARINADE

Ingredients

bunch of flat-leaf parsley
120ml (4fl oz) olive oil
2 tbsp balsamic vinegar
2 tbsp crushed garlic
1 large red onion, finely chopped
sea salt
freshly ground black pepper

1 Roughly chop the parsley, reserving half for garnish.

2 In a large bowl, whisk the oil, balsamic vinegar, garlic, red onion, and half the parsley. Add salt and pepper to taste.

3 Place the mushroom caps in a zip-lock plastic food bag, and completely cover with marinade. Put in the refrigerator to marinate overnight. Drain before smoking.

TIME PLAN (9¾–11¾ HRS)

40 mins	8–10 hrs		30 mins	30 mins	5 mins
Prep	Marinate		Build the fire	Smoke	Rest

> I garnish mushroom caps with the flat-leaf parsley, a little grated Parmesan or Asiago cheese, and a small splash of balsamic vinegar. You could stuff them with rice and vegetables for a heartier main course. 〝

))) THE SMOKE

1 With the pit temperature stabilized at 121°C (250°F), add an additional log to the fire and close all the vents. The goal is to have a heavy smoke fill the smoker chamber.

2 Use tongs to place the mushrooms, gills up, in the middle of the pit and away from any hot spots.

3 Allow to smoke, without turning, for 30 minutes, or until tender when pierced with a fork.

4 Remove from the pit and allow to rest uncovered for 5 minutes. Garnish with the remaining parsley.

Side Asparagus	Wood Oak	Prep time 40 mins	Smoker temp 121°C (250°F)	Cook time 30 mins	Rest time None	Yield Serves 4

When in season, asparagus is a fabulous vegetable. Its mild flavour and hearty texture responds well to being smoked because it doesn't break down and become mushy on the smoker, as some other vegetables can.

SMOKED ASPARAGUS with PORK BELLY

 ## THE SIDE

Bunch of asparagus

• Buy asparagus that is fresh-cut, avoiding any stems that have signs of browning on the cut ends.

• The narrower the stalk, the more tender the asparagus, so look for stalks that are about the thickness of a wooden pencil. Larger stalks can be reedy and fibrous and have an unpleasant texture.

 ## THE FIRE

Light the pit fire 1 hour before smoking. Add wood 30 minutes before smoking.

• Target temp: 121°C (250°F)

• Wood needs: Low

THE PREP

Ingredients

½ lemon
60g (2oz) unsalted butter, cut into slices
½ tbsp crushed garlic
sea salt
115g (4oz) smoked pork belly, diced

1 Remove the seeds from the lemon, if necessary. Set aside.

2 Break the bases from the asparagus stalks: bend them and allow them to break at a natural point of weakness (as opposed to cutting them off uniformly with a knife).

3 On a large piece of heavy-duty foil, arrange the asparagus stalks evenly.

4 Top the asparagus with the butter slices, garlic, salt, and pieces of smoked pork belly. (Pork belly adds saltiness, so be gentle when adding salt.) Fold the edges of the foil to form a pouch, but don't seal the top.

THE SMOKE

1 With the pit temperature stabilized at 121°C (250°F), place the pouch of asparagus onto any available pit space.

2 Smoke for 30 minutes or until one of the thicker stems is tender when pierced by a fork.

3 Take the asparagus from the pit, then remove the stalks from the foil. Add a squeeze of lemon and serve immediately.

TIME PLAN (1 HR 40 MINS)

30 mins	40 mins	30 mins
Build the fire	Prep	Smoke

I FINISH THE ASPARAGUS BY SQUEEZING LEMON JUICE OVER TOP AND EVENLY DISTRIBUTING THE SMOKED PORK BELLY AMONG THE STALKS.

Side Mushroom	**Wood** Oak	**Prep time** 30 mins	**Smoker temp** 121°C (250°F)	**Cook time** 20–30 mins	**Rest time** None	**Yield** Serves 4

This sweet-and-bitter salad is a great complement to a heavy meat such as beef. The sweet grapes work in stark contrast to the intense flavour of smoked dark ale.

SMOKED WILD MUSHROOM and WHITE GRAPE SALAD

THE SIDE

300–350g (10–12 oz) wild mushrooms

• Any variety of in-season and fresh wild mushrooms you can find, such as ceps, chanterelles, morels, or even field mushrooms or giant puff balls, take smoke flavours very well and will become tender and robustly smoked after 20 minutes in the pit. Cut up large wild mushrooms so all pieces are of a fairly even size.

THE FIRE

Light the pit fire 1 hour before smoking. Add wood 30 minutes before smoking.

• Target temp: 121°C (250°F)
• Wood needs: Low

THE DRESSING

Ingredients

90ml (3fl oz) balsamic vinegar
dash of mustard powder
pinch of sea salt
1 tsp granulated sugar
175ml (6fl oz) olive oil
300g (10oz) white grapes, halved
240ml (8fl oz) dark ale of your choice

1 In a medium bowl, whisk together the vinegar, mustard powder, salt, sugar, and olive oil until emulsified. Set aside.

2 Place the grapes in a large bowl. Set aside. Pour the ale into a small flame- and ovenproof heavy-based saucepan. Set aside.

3 Place the wild mushrooms in a lage piece of heavy-duty foil. Fold the edges of the foil to form a pouch, but don't seal the top.

THE SMOKE

1 With the pit temperature at 121°C (250°F), place the wild mushroom pouch and the pan of dark ale into the middle of the pit.

2 Smoke for 20–30 minutes, or until the mushrooms are tender when pierced by a fork.

3 Remove the smoked ale from the pit and pour into the dressing. Mix well to re-emulsify.

4 Combine the smoked mushrooms straight from the pit with the grapes.

5 Drizzle the mushrooms and grapes with the dressing and serve immediately.

TIME PLAN (1 HR 25 MINS TO 1 HR 35 MINS)

30 mins	30 mins	20–30 mins	5 mins
Build the fire	Prep	Smoke	Dress the salad

Side	Wood	Prep time	Smoker temp	Cook time	Rest time	Yield
Tomatillo and serrano chillies	Oak	20 mins	121°C (250°F)	30 mins	20 mins	500ml (16fl oz)

This will soon be a staple item in your kitchen. It's easy to make, a real talking point, and brings a refreshing bite to almost any smoked meat, particularly pork or poultry.

SMOKED TOMATILLO SALSA

THE SIDE

5–6 tomatillos (available online or from speciality shops), peeled and finely chopped

THE FIRE

Light the pit fire 1 hour before smoking. Add wood 30 minutes before smoking.

- Target temp: 121°C (250°F)
- Wood needs: Low

A VERDANT SAUCE
The crisp lime juice, the aromatic coriander, and the slight bite of the serrano chillies make this salsa a delicious – and colourful – accompaniment to any barbecue feast. It can also dress up any leftover barbecue meat you roll up in a tortilla wrap.

THE PREP

Ingredients

2 serrano chillies, deseeded and finely chopped
1/2 white onion, finely chopped
pinch of sea salt
juice of 1/2 lime
5–6 sprigs of fresh coriander, roughly chopped
white wine vinegar (optional)

1 In a shallow flame- and ovenproof heavy-based saucepan, combine the tomatillos, serrano chillies, onion, and salt. Set aside.

2 Place the lime juice, coriander, and vinegar (if using) in separate bowls. Set aside.

" **This salsa is made from sweet-sharp tomatillos, and will probably be a new, exciting taste for your guests.** "

THE SMOKE

1 With the pit temperature stabilized at 121°C (250°F), place the pan into the smoker wherever you have room.

2 Allow the tomatillos, serrano chillies, and onion to smoke for about 30 minutes, or until the tomatillos and onion have an attractive smoky brown appearance and the chillies are tinged with smoke on their edges.

3 Remove the pan from the smoker. Add the lime juice, mixture and combine.

4 Transfer the salsa to an airtight container and refrigerate until cool, about 20 minutes. Adjust the amount of salt to taste. This will keep in the refrigerator for up to 1 week.

TIME PLAN (1 HR 50 MINS)

30 mins	20 mins	30 mins	10 mins	20 mins
Build the fire	Prep	Smoke	Combine	Rest

Side Habanero	Wood Oak	Prep time 50 mins	Smoker temp 121°C (250°F)	Cook time 35 mins	Rest time 2 days	Yield 1.7 litres (3 pints)

Hot sauce is a guilty pleasure for many barbecue cooks. The sweet, fruity fragrance and eye-opening, sweat-inducing heat of this variety make for a beautiful combination.

SMOKED HABANERO HOT SAUCE

THE SIDE

8–10 habanero peppers

THE FIRE

Light the pit fire 1 hour before smoking. Add wood 30 minutes before smoking.

- Target temp: 121°C (250°F)
- Wood needs: Low

ALWAYS WEAR GLOVES!
You'll definitely need to wear disposable gloves while you're handling fresh habaneros. Not wearing gloves can lead to quite a bit of discomfort, as many painful and eye-watering episodes of making this hot sauce have taught me.

THE PREP

1 While wearing disposable plastic gloves, remove the stems from the habaneros.

2 Cut in half lengthways and arrange in a large flame- and ovenproof heavy-based saucepan.

THE SAUCE

Ingredients

1.4 litres (2½ pints) white wine vinegar
200g (7oz) granulated sugar
3 tbsp sea salt
1 tbsp mustard powder
120ml (4fl oz) orange juice or pineapple juice

1 In a large bowl, whisk together the vinegar, sugar, salt, mustard powder, and juice. Set aside.

THE SMOKE

1 With the pit temperature stabilized at 121°C (250°F), place the saucepan in the smoker.

2 Allow the habaneros to smoke until they begin to smell sweet and fragrant, about 35 minutes. Remove from the pit and rest until cool to the touch.

3 Working in batches and wearing disposable plastic gloves, place the habaneros in a food processor and pulse on high until fully blended. Mix with all the other ingredients.

4 Place in a sealed non-reactive container and store in the refrigerator for at least 2 days. This allows the flavours to meld and the colour to become brilliant orange. Keep for up to 1 month.

TIME PLAN (2 DAYS 2 HRS 5 MINS)

30 mins	50 mins	35 mins	20 mins	2 days
Build the fire	Prep	Smoke	Blend	Rest

KITCHEN SAFETY

It goes without saying that using common sense around smokers and in your kitchen must be the norm. By observing these simple smoker and kitchen rules, you'll stay safe, smoke more delicious foods, and enjoy a more enriched smoking experience.

SMOKER SAFETY RULES

- Test a surface for how hot it is by putting your hand 5–7.5cm (2–3in) above it. If it feels hot from that distance, it can burn… and if it can burn, it can hurt you.

- Allow hot ash to sufficiently cool down before removing it from your pit or throwing it away. You'll save a lot of containers if you give burning-hot ash a bit of cooling time.

- Don't use artificial accelerants on your fire. Allow the charcoal and wood to reduce to coals and feed them fuel over time in small amounts.

- Be aware of your overhead surroundings. Dry leaves or brush can catch fire from the embers wafting from your smoker.

- Be aware of where your smoker is placed in relationship to your house, or to property fences. Hot coals and a hot pit can still cause smoke damage and heat damage.

- Cook food to a recommended internal temperature of 77°C (170°F). This should kill all bacteria, parasites, and viruses, thereby helping to prevent any food-related illnesses.

- Always use an instant-read thermometer to check internal temperatures. Never rely just on sight or touch to gauge the doneness of the meats you're smoking until you gain experience.

- Keep pets and children away from the pit's firebox. After all, you don't want to put a damper on a fun get-together due to a child or animal getting hurt by the pit.

FOOD-HANDLING KITCHEN RULES

- Store all raw meat and fish at the bottom of the refrigerator. This prevents any juices from dripping onto other foods and thus causing serious food-related illnesses.

- Cool foods in your refrigerator, not at room temperature, to ensure they reach ideal serving temperatures quickly without the threat of bacteria.

- Thaw frozen foods in your refrigerator, in your microwave, or under cold running water rather than at room temperature, so bacteria doesn't grow.

- Don't use the same chopping board for different foods during preparation. You can avoid cross-contamination by using specific boards for specific foods, but if you have more foods than boards, your best bet is to thoroughly wash your chopping boards between each use, regardless of what's been on them.

- Heat leftovers to at least 77°C (170°F). This ensures any microbes that are in cold food will be killed.

- Wash your hands for at least 20 seconds – using soap and hot water – after touching any raw meat or any surface where you've prepared it. Quickly clean any surfaces that have been in contact with raw meat.

- Store food at below 4°C (40°F) or above 60°C (140°F), and never keep leftovers in your refrigerator for longer than 7 days. If you need to keep something stored for longer, put it in the freezer and try to eat it within a few months.

- Consider using disposable latex or vinyl gloves when handling food.

- Buy your food from reputable sources. Make sure anything you buy comes with information about its origins.

- Throw out any food that seems suspicious, whether it has a funny smell, looks spoiled, or anything else about it that seems unusual. You're better safe than sorry by throwing something out than risking cooking or eating it.

GLOSSARY

Bark The delicious, crispy, dark outer layer that forms on meats that are smoked low and slow.

Baste Brushing with pan drippings, a sauce, or another kind of liquid to help food keep its moisture while cooking. Most basting is done with a brush or a mop, which is also another term for this process.

Brine A water and salt solution most commonly used to add flavour and moisture to poultry. When it is left to soak in a brine overnight, a chemical exchange occurs that draws seasoning into the fibres and adds moisture.

Residual cooking The continued rise in the internal temperature of a meat after it has been removed from the smoker. This cooking could mean a temperature increase of as little as 1°C (2°F) or as much as 5°C (10°F) , depending on the cut, which can make the crucial difference between rare and medium.

Charcoal The common name for fuel used to start the fire in a smoker or a grill. The wide variety of commercial brands use accelerants and chemicals to create heat and can impart strange aromas and tastes to your food, so use an all-natural product instead.

Coals The glowing remains of wood and charcoal that produce the heat for cooking.

Cooking chamber The area of the smoker where the foods are placed for cooking.

Dip A thin sauce you dunk meat into after it's been cooked. These dips often use tomato, vinegar, or mustard bases.

Direct cooking The process of cooking a food directly over the heat source. Also known as grilling.

Firebox Regardless of the smoker's configuration, the area that holds the coals and cooking wood, and where heat and smoke are produced.

Indirect cooking The process of cooking with a heat source that's not directly under the food.

Lump charcoal Carbonized wood that's typically derived from hardwood trees. The ideal choice for fuel, it doesn't contain the chemical additives that commercial charcoal contains, and burns at a high temperature.

Marinate The process of putting uncooked meat in a sauce, liquid, or a rub overnight, or for an extended period of time. This is usually done to infuse a food with a flavour, but it can also help make it more tender and allow it to cook more easily.

Mop Used as a noun, this is the device used to slather liquid onto a protein. Used as a verb, it's the act of applying the sauce itself (the same as basting).

Render The process of breaking down fat and changing it into a liquid state.

Rest The period of time meats need to be left alone before being put on the smoker, as well as after cooking and before carving.

Rub A mix of dry seasonings applied to meats that interacts with the smoke to create the delicious outer bark, and that also aids in the formation of the smoke ring.

Sauce A liquid that can be vinegar-based, ketchup-based, or mustard-based and applied to foods as a seasoning additive. (Barbecue sauce has been loved or loathed by smoker cooks for generations, and recipes are often coveted family secrets.)

Sear A process that doesn't actually cook the meat through but instead creates a caramelization on its surface. You use direct heat on a meat to sear it. You can also "reverse sear" a meat, which means cooking over indirect heat before searing it.

Smoke ring The red-to-mahogany coloured line that forms inside proteins. To many aficionados, this is the gold standard of great smoked meats. The smoke ring forms when amino acids in the foods react with the carbon in smoke.

Smoker Also referred to as a *pit,* a device that holds meats away from a heat source for indirect cooking.

SMOKING TIMES AND TEMPS

BEEF

Beef presents a range of doneness levels that can be adjusted to fit your taste preferences.

MEAT	DONENESS LEVEL	COOK TIME	PULL TEMP	SERVING TEMP
Brisket	Well	12–14 hrs	77°C (170°F)	82°C (180°F)
Ribeye	Rare	28 mins	57°C (135°F)	60°C (140°F)
	Medium-rare	30 mins	60°C (140°F)	63°C (145°F)
	Medium	35 mins	68°C (155°F)	71°C (160°F)
	Medium-well	40 mins	74°C (165°F)	77°C (170°F)
Short ribs	Well	8–9 hrs	93°C (200°F)	96°C (205°F)
Shoulder (clod)	Well	18–20 hrs	79°C (175°F)	82°C (180°F)
Fillet	Medium-rare	45 mins	63°C (145°F)	63°C (145°F)
	Medium	1 hr	71°C (160°F)	71°C (160°F)

GAME

The optimal doneness level for game depends on both the type of game you're smoking and the cut.

MEAT	DONENESS LEVEL	COOK TIME	PULL TEMP	SERVING TEMP
Bison ribeye	Rare	40 mins	57°C (135°F)	60°C (140°F)
Elk fillet	Rare	50 mins	52°C (125°F)	54°C (130°F)
	Medium-rare	1 hr	57°C (135°F)	60°C (140°F)
	Medium	1½ hrs	60°C (140°F)	66°C (150°F)
Venison tenderloin	Rare	40 mins	57°C (135°F)	60°C (140°F)
	Medium-rare	50 mins	58°C (136°F)	61°C (141°F)
Whole pheasant	Medium	4–4½ hrs	71°C (160°F)	74°C (165°F)
Wild boar ribs	Well	3½–4 hrs	77°C (170°F)	82°C (180°F)

LAMB

Lamb presents a range of doneness levels that can be adjusted to fit your taste preferences.

MEAT	DONENESS LEVEL	COOK TIME	PULL TEMP	SERVING TEMP
Lamb necks	Well	5½ hrs	74°C (165°F)	77°C (170°F)
Lamb shanks	Well	3½ hrs	74°C (165°F)	77°C (170°F)
Rack of lamb	Rare	45 mins	54°C (130°F)	57°C (135°F)
	Medium-rare	1 hr	60°C (140°F)	63°C (145°F)
	Medium	1¼ hrs	68°C (155°F)	71°C (160°F)

PORK

While pork should always be cooked through completely, the temperature range will vary based on the cut.

MEAT	DONENESS LEVEL	COOK TIME	PULL TEMP	SERVING TEMP
Baby back ribs	Well	3½–4 hrs	77°C (170°F)	77°C (170°F)
Ham	Well	3 hrs	66°C (150°F)	71°C (160°F)
Pork belly	Well	1½ hrs	71°C (160°F)	77°C (170°F)
Pulled pork shoulder	Well	5½ hrs	91°C (195°F)	91°C (195°F)
Spare ribs	Well	4–5 hrs	77°C (170°F)	82°C (180°F)

POULTRY

Poultry should always be cooked through completely and to a minimum of 74°C (165°F).

MEAT	DONENESS LEVEL	COOK TIME	PULL TEMP	SERVING TEMP
Chicken thighs	Well	2½–3 hrs	71°C (160°F) to 74°C (165°F)	77°C (170°F)
Chicken wings	Well	1½ hrs	79°C (175°F)	82°C (180°F)
Jumbo chicken wings	Well	2 hrs 5 mins	74°C (165°F)	74°C (165°F)
Quail	Well	45 mins	71°C (160°F)	74°C (165°F)
Turkey breast	Well	4 hrs	71°C (160°F)	82°C (180°F)
Whole chicken	Well	4½ hrs	74°C (165°F)	77°C (170°F)

INDEX

ABOUT THE AUTHOR

Will Fleischman is an award-winning Texas pitmaster, brand ambassador for Black Iron BBQ Pits, and the co-creator of Bare Knuckle Premium Rubs. Prior to tending pits in Texas, Will was a chef in China, a college professor, and the owner of several small businesses. But smoking meat was – and is – his calling. Will's brisket has been sampled by Andrew Zimmern on the Travel Channel's *Bizarre Foods America* and was featured when Will was a competitor on Season 4 of Destination America's *BBQ Pitmasters*. In 2012, he was named one of the 10 best pitmasters in the American South by *Southern Living* magazine.

ACKNOWLEDGMENTS

Throughout my BBQ life, many people have been instrumental in encouraging me, challenging me, and providing feedback on my food and crazy ideas. And others have brought crazy ideas of their own. Eric Perry, a renowned knuckle-dragger and generally a BBQ badass, has been a constant muse and partner in crime. Big E has worked with me on developing recipes and creating flavour profiles that pack a punch and leave lasting impressions.

Eric's wife (The Good Wife, or TGW) has been patient throughout as we've cluttered their back yard with our various and sundry experiments and constant clouds of smoke. Thanks for being my second home.

Black Iron BBQ Pits has been a great supporter of this project, providing a Pit Viper smoker, custom tools, and prep tables that made the food preparation and execution of the recipes found in this book a cool breeze. Thanks to Greg and David for the opportunity to form this ongoing confederacy.

The willingness of Tim McLaughlin and Jeff Bergus to give me a chance to cook BBQ in their restaurant – and their patience and their chequebooks – really helped me find this professional niche. It's been a wild ride, fellas.

And to the stream of friends, girlfriends, and total strangers who have meandered through my BBQ life, thanks for the arguments, hassles, encouragement, and support. Here's to many more years of smoke-filled fun and great food!

DK USA
Publisher Mike Sanders
Associate Publisher Billy Fields
Senior Acquisitions Editor Brook Farling
Development Editors Kayla Dugger and Christopher Stolle
Designer Hannah Moore
Illustrator Philippa Nash
Photographer Joy Zhang
Food Stylist Angela Yeung
Recipe Tester Matt Gatesy
Proofreader Laura Caddell
Indexer Heather McNeill

DK UK
Angliciser and Editor Lucy Bannell
Project Editor Kathryn Meeker
Senior Art Editor Glenda Fisher
Jacket Designer Nicola Powling
Pre-production Producer Andy Hilliard
Senior Producer Stephanie McConnell
Creative Technical Support Sonia Charbonnier
Managing Editor Stephanie Farrow
Managing Art Editor Christine Keilty

First published in Great Britain in 2016 by
Dorling Kindersley Limited
80 Strand, London, WC2R 0RL

Copyright © 2016 Dorling Kindersley Limited
A Penguin Random House Company
10 9 8 7 6 5 4 3 2 1
001–290929–May/2016

A CIP catalogue record for this book is available from the British Library.
ISBN: 978-0-2412-4828-7

Printed and bound in Slovakia

All images © Dorling Kindersley Limited
For further information see: www.dkimages.com

A WORLD OF IDEAS:
SEE ALL THERE IS TO KNOW